HOW TO TAILOR

How to TAILOR

A HANDBOOK FOR HOME TAILORING

by

PHYLLIS W. SCHWEBKE

REVISED EDITION

THE BRUCE PUBLISHING COMPANY,
NEW YORK
COLLIER-MACMILLAN, LIMITED, LONDON

Library of Congress Catalog Card Number: 65-19749

THE BRUCE PUBLISHING COMPANY, NEW YORK
COLLIER-MACMILLAN CANADA, LTD., TORONTO, ONTARIO

MADE IN THE UNITED STATES OF AMERICA

Foreword

THIS handbook has been written to assist the student and home sewer with her tailoring problems, particularly in the construction of coats, suits, and men's sport coats. The home sewer may be a college girl, homemaker, or career girl who is tailoring her first suit or who has tailored and would like to employ some "tricks of the trade" to accomplish the custom-tailored look. This book may be used at home, in the adult-education classroom, as well as at the college level. As far as possible, the book is arranged in logical sequence for ease in use.

It has been assumed that the person who tailors has had much experience in dressmaking — that she can handle material, follow basic directions, is skillful in stitching, and can press well.

Since this is a technical book, the sentences are concise and brief. A new outline form, borrowed from industry's job sheet and highly approved by those who have tested it, has been used in this tailoring manual.

All basic tailoring operations are presented in step-by-step form and are supplemented by diagrams where necessary. When more than one method is discussed, it may be assumed that the first one is preferred by the author. In some cases, you will notice differences between dressmaking techniques and those used by the tailor. An experienced person may well try the tailor's methods, but the beginner may prefer the approved dressmaker methods.

There is a general procedure sheet inside the back cover for each of the following types of garments: suit jacket or coat (with the lining sewn in by hand), suit jacket or coat and men's jackets (with part of the lining sewn in by machine), garments with shawl collars and skirts. Select the procedure you will use; then follow it step by step to complete the garment, referring to the sections as indicated for additional information.

The author is indebted to her former teachers of tailoring: Prof. Hazel Van Ness and Prof. Lillian Jeter, formerly of Stout State University; Mr. Herbert W. Rieger, formerly of Milwaukee Vocational and Adult School; and Mr. Peter Simmons, a tailor in Madison, Wisconsin, who was educated in England. Deep gratitude should also be expressed to Mrs. Hazel Paschall, Associate Professor of Textiles and Clothing at The University of Wisconsin, for her encouragement, suggestions, and advice during the writing of this handbook. The author wishes to thank her husband, Prof. Howard Schwebke for doing the original drawings and Mrs. Virginia Goplen for inspiring the fashion sketches. Also, the author would like to express her appreciation to the tailoring students in her classes during the years this book was being written and tested. It was through their interest and enthusiasm that it reached its completion. Lastly, to her husband and sons, John and James, she owes gratitude for their loyal support and encouragement during this endeavor.

This material has been tested by tailoring classes held at the Madison Vocational and Adult School in Madison, Wisconsin, with the permission of Miss Winifred Layden, formerly the Homemaking Supervisor there, and Mr. Richard Bardwell, formerly the Director. It was also used in the tailoring classes in the Monona Grove Adult Evening School program in Madison, Wisconsin.

Contents

CONTENTS

Chapter

CHAPTER 1

Types of Tailoring

SINCE many types of tailoring are used today, the home sewer should understand the differences between them. "Tailoring" means advanced sewing combined with some special techniques with precision and accuracy for constructing suits and coats. Three types of tailored garments may be distinguished.

First, there is the *custom-tailored* garment which is constructed to fit the individual after her or his measurements have been taken. The material and findings in this case are selected for the particular garment. This type of tailoring involves much handwork; therefore, the cost is high, but the garment fits superbly and holds its shape well. This is the type of tailoring to be discussed in this handbook.

Many stores feature a *made-to-order* type of garment for which the measurements of the individual are taken and the garment is factory made. The garment will usually fit fairly well, but it involves less handwork and the price is less than that of a custom-tailored one.

Third, there is the *ready-made* suit tailored to a standard size, which is factory made by pattern with no individual purchaser in mind. If a person is of normal stature and symmetry, this garment may fit satisfactorily or may be altered to fit properly. This garment costs the least of the three types mentioned.

The home sewer may construct a strictly custom-tailored garment with "custom-tailoring" methods, or she may use a combination of tailoring (both

custom and mass production) and dressmaking techniques. The short-cut method of tailoring is an example of the latter type where many simplified processes are employed. These methods could be used for children's garments which are worn for a relatively short time, for unlined garments, dressmaker types of suits, and for the homemaker who has little time to devote to tailoring. Custom tailoring techniques can be used by the home sewer for notched collared (tailored) suit styles, men's sport coats, and coats.

Coats and suits represent the bulk in expense in the family's clothing budget. These garments usually can be constructed at home for less than half of the purchase price of a ready-made garment. This does not take into consideration the value of time. From this viewpoint, many feel that the time and energy are "well spent" for, if skillfully done, the garment is a work of art. One should allow sufficient time to make the tailored garment and work accurately.

The custom-tailored garment will have thin edges, which are straight. The grain will be perfect, the lining loose and not pulled, with a smooth fit throughout the garment. For more details in fit see Chapter 41, "Characteristics of the Garment With a 'Custom Look.'"

Will you, as a home sewer, follow the step-by-step directions in this handbook and construct a custom-tailored garment? Follow the procedural outline inside the back cover of the book.

CHAPTER 2

Terms and Phrases Used in Tailoring

THERE are many phrases and terms which are commonly used in custom tailoring but may be new to the novice. One should become familiar with these terms in order to understand the procedures used in tailoring. It may be necessary to refer to this glossary.

Armscye. An armhole.

Arrowhead. A tack stitch used to reinforce and decorate the ends of pockets, pleats, etc. (Fig. 62).

Backstitch. A stitch used for strong seams or edge finishing of bulky garments. The needle is inserted and pushed through from the wrong side at a diagonal, followed by a backstitch, working toward the left (Fig. 63).

Bar tack. A bar made to reinforce the ends of pockets, plackets, or stitching lines on pleats (Fig. 65).

Bias.

True — The exact 45-deg. diagonal of the material. At this point the fabric has the most "give" (Fig. 1, A–B).

Garment — Any diagonal direction of fabric (Fig. 1, A–C and A–D).

Breakline or creaseline. The folded edge of the lapel, as the revers turns back over the coat front (Fig. 2, A–B).

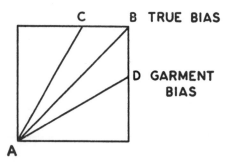

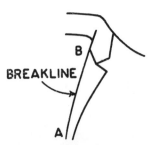

Fig. 2. Breakline or creaseline.

Bridle. A strip of tape or unstretchable material sewed on the canvas along or just behind the breakline fold or creaseline (Fig. 3, A–B). This prevents that line from stretching and insures better fit over the bustline.

Fig. 3. Bridle.

Build a coat. The tailoring or construction of a coat.

Canvas. A linen, cotton, wool, or hair fabric, of firm weave used to interface the coat front. In a man's garment it may refer to a completed interfacing which has several layers of fabric at the shoulder area.

Catch stitch. A cross-stitch made by working from left to right. It is used to hold two pieces of fabric together smoothly, yet allows flexibility. It is often used when overlapping the seams of interfacing (Fig. 66).

Cloth. A term referring to the material of which the garment is tailored.

Fig. 1. True bias and garment bias.

Collar. See Figure 4.

Creaseline — The uppermost folded edge of the collar.

Fall or leaf edge — The part of the collar which comes between the crease-line and the outer edge of the collar.

Stand — The part of the collar between the creaseline and the neck edge.

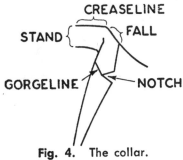

Fig. 4. The collar.

Cotton felt. A firm, heavy, felted cotton used around the armscye and for extra padding when fitting hollows.

Custom look. An expression used with reference to a garment that has the appearance of being hand tailored to fit the individual.

Design allowance. Extra ease in a pattern resulting from gathers, tucks, shirrings, and bloused effects.

Ease thread or drawing-in thread. A fine running stitch along a seamline used to ease a longer section to a shorter edge, as the back shoulder to the front, the sleeve cap to the armhole; or, used at the lower armscye before shaping.

Felling. A tailor's version of slant hemming, or sewing toward oneself. The stitches should be even, fine, and shallow, but not too tight. It is used to attach linen tape to the canvas and the undercollar to the coat.

Findings. Supplies in addition to the wool fabric and lining needed to tailor a garment; selecting trimmings (see page 19).

Fish dart. A dart tapered at both ends.

Fly front. A type of closing which conceals the buttons or a zipper.

Forepart. Left and right fronts of a coat.

Fulling on. Easing a longer length of material onto a shorter length.

Gimp. A heavy thread used to pad tailored worked buttonholes.

Gorgeline. The part of the seamline that joins the collar and the facing extending from the creaseline to the notch (Fig. 5).

Grading seams. Trimming seam edges,

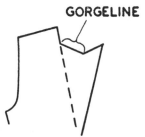

Fig. 5. Gorgeline.

one shorter than the other, to eliminate bulk. For example, when joining the facing to the coat, trim the coat seam to ¼ in. and the facing seam shorter so that the wider seam edge will lie against the outside surface of the coat.

Grain. A term referring to the filling yarns (crosswise) running perpendicular to the selvage and warp yarns (lengthwise) running parallel to the selvage.

Ham-shaped cushion. A pressing cushion used for molding curved and shaped areas, such as sleeve edges, bustline, etc.

Hard tailoring. A term referring to man-tailored garments.

Hymo. A hair canvas interfacing used for reinforcing the body of the garment.

Inlay. Extra allowance added to seams for enlargement of the garment.

Interfacing or reinforcement. A fabric such as hymo, linen canvas, wigan, pellon, or muslin used to give body to material and help it hold its shape.

Interlining. A fabric placed between the lining and the coat material for added warmth, such as wool, chamois, outing flannel, etc.

Jumping. Patting two thicknesses of wool together to smooth it.

Lapel. The front edge of the coat.

Laying on fair. Sewing two seams or lengths together so the ends are even.

Laying up the cloth. Placing the material on the table for cutting.

Melton. Firm, nonfraying napped twilled wool fabric used for undercollar cloth on tailored garments, especially for men's tailored garments.

Mouthline. The finished opening of the pocket.

Nap. Hairy or downy surface on fabric. Examples: broadcloth, flannel, and duvetyn.

Notch. The area from the end of the gorgeline to the point of the collar end (Fig. 4).

On the double. The folded material as it comes from the bolt.

Overcasting. Over-and-over stitch used to finish raw edges to keep them from fraying.

Pad stitch. Used for fastening canvas to the facing of the revers, the collar canvas onto the undercollar, or the hair cloth to the canvas interlining on men's garments. It is worked from the interfacing side but does not show through on the right side. On the inside of the garment, the padding appears as parallel rows of diagonal stitches.

Permanent basting. Any type of basting using matching thread which remains in the finished garment.

Pile. A velvety surface produced by extra filling yarns cut and sheared. Examples: velvets, velveteens, corduroys.

Pitch of sleeve. The angle at which the sleeve falls from the armhole.

Plumb. A weight attached to a line to indicate true vertical direction, i.e., the side seams of a garment.

Pocket facing. A piece of garment fabric attached to the pocketing, so that wool shows when the pocket is used, rather than the lining.

Pocket stay. A strip of wigan, muslin, or linen, used on the wrong side of the coat fabric to reinforce the mouthline.

Pouch. The pocket lining itself.

Purl. The knot portion of the buttonhole stitch.

Revers. The turned-over portion of the coat front.

Saddle stitch. A hand stitch used near the edge of garment for a decorative effect. A coarse thread and long stitches are characteristic of this stitch.

Scye. The armhole; often, armscye.

Silesia. Pocket twill used for pocket pouches.

Skeleton lining. Any lining that is not a complete lining used in a man's suit coat.

Skive. To cut off a portion of cloth at an angle.

Spanking. Pounding or flattening the edges of the wool with heat and steam when it is moist.

Stab stitch. A stitch in which the needle goes straight through the material at right angles and returns the same way. It may be used for edge finishing, sewing on buttons, and attaching shoulder pads at the seamline.

Stays. Any unstretchable material, such as muslin, wigan, or linen used for reinforcement.

Swing tack (French tack). A stitch used to hold fabrics fairly close together but free, for example, the coat lining to the hem of the garment. The tack consists of threads showing about ¼ to ½ in. in length with bar covering it completely.

Tailor or diagonal basting. Short parallel stitches with long diagonal threads showing about 1 to 3 in. in length, used to hold the reinforcement and the coat together.

Tailor tacks. Used to mark perforations on materials on which a tracing wheel cannot be used effectively.

Top stitching. Machine stitching showing on the right side of the garment. Sometimes called surface stitching.

Trimmings (findings). Anything in addition to cloth used in a garment.

Underlining. A lining cut like the garment cloth. The two are treated as one when stitching; this gives support and shape to the garment.

Under pocket lining. The part of the lining pouch which falls next to the lining of the garment.

Upper pocket lining. The part of the lining pouch which falls next to the outside of the garment.

Vent. A lapped finished opening at the bottom of the center back or sides of the coat, or on the sleeves.

Welt. A strip of material used to finish the lower edge of the mouthline of a pocket.

Wigan. A cotton material used for reinforcement of cuffs, jacket bottom, back, pocket stays, etc.

Zigzag stitch. A stitch used to join two edges of reinforcements. It may be done on a zigzag-type sewing machine, or with an attachment, or by lifting the reverse stitching bar on a machine that sews backward (Fig. 6).

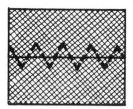

Fig. 6. A zigzag stitch.

CHAPTER **3**

Equipment Used in Tailoring

THERE are many pieces of equipment used in tailoring in the classroom that may not be readily available at home. Satisfactory substitutes may be used for some of these articles, or the equipment can be constructed easily in the home workshop. Below is a list of essential tailoring equipment. Many of the items are used in dressmaking. Those marked with an asterisk (*) can be constructed at home. The equipment can also be purchased at a tailor's supply house.

Equipment

Basting thread. Darning cotton, embroidery thread, or double-duty mercerized thread in size 40 is desirable; however, contrasting thread from the home sewing basket may be used.

*Beater. A shaped block made of heavy hardwood and used uncovered to flatten seams without shine (Fig. 9). The beater is grooved for convenient handling. It should not be finished. Softwood is not recommended because heat may cause the sap to come to the surface. Also called a *pounding block, clapper,* or *spanker.*

Beeswax. Wax through which thread is pulled and smoothed to prevent knotting.

Bodkin. A bone or plastic instrument with a rounded point used for turning notched revers and removing bastings.

Buttonhole cutter. A type of scissors used for cutting buttonholes. An ordinary scissors or sharp single-edged razor blade may be substituted for it.

*Cheese block. A wooden block in the shape of a half circle, 2 to 3 in. thick, used for pressing flat and curved surfaces (Fig. 10). It should be made of

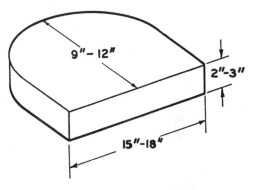

Fig. 10. A cheese block.

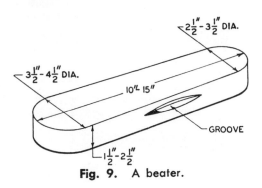

Fig. 9. A beater.

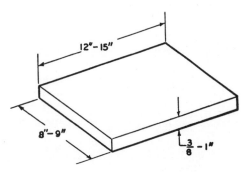

Fig. 11. A wood press-block.

white oak, maple, birch, or other hardwood. It may be used uncovered as it leaves the wool surface flat and the appearance unchanged. Sometimes the tailor uses a wood press block for long seams (Fig. 11). Occasionally a cheese block may be covered with two layers of felt and muslin for pressing.

*Edge presser. A narrow, unfinished wooden piece of pressing equipment, which has no covering and is used to press open the seams of collars, lapels, coat-facing seams, etc. (Fig. 12).

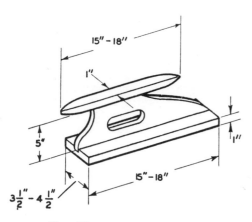

Fig. 12.   An edge presser.

Form. A replica of a figure on which garments are placed when putting in the lining, setting in the sleeves, or putting on collars.

Gauge. A metal 6-in. ruler with a slide marker, which is handy for all measuring. A metal gauge is recommended, but a cardboard one may be made, or one of plastic may be purchased.

Hem marker. A mounted measuring stick with an adjustable metal arm which is effective for hanging skirt or coat hems. A yardstick may be substituted for it.

Iron. A tailor's flatiron usually weighs from 8 to 15 lb.; however, an ordinary household or steam iron may be used successfully.

Ironing board. A regulation ironing board is a convenience.

Mirror. A full-length mirror is desirable.

Needles. Tailors use "betweens," which are short and have round eyes. No. 3–5's are desirable for basting and No. 6 for hand sewing with silk thread.

Pins. Dressmaker pins, sizes 15, 16, or 17, can be purchased by the box.

*Press cloth. A thick cloth of drill is used by many for pressing wool. It should be thoroughly washed to remove sizing. The tailor often uses a lightweight wool or cotton silence cloth with a cotton cloth or drill sewed on top, about 18 by 36 in. or 9 to 24 in. in size. When this is used, a wet cloth is laid on top or it is sponged with water. Some use a drawstring fitted cloth over the bottom of a steam iron or a commercial chemically treated cloth. Several layers of cheesecloth or a single layer of linen, because it is lintless, may also be used.

*Press mitt. A small mitt with a pocket in which the hand is inserted. It is used in pressing the top of the sleeves. It may be purchased or made of heavy cotton fabric or drill, and filled with cotton batting, sawdust, or wool (Fig. 13).

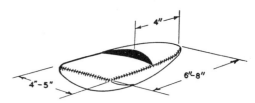

Fig. 13.   A press mitt.

Ruler. An 18-in. ruler or yardstick is handy for checking the perfection of grain.

Scissors. A rip-stitch scissors is handy for ripping. Regular sewing scissors are used for clipping threads at the machine or when doing hand sewing.

*Seam roll. A pressing pad for pressing seams. It may be made by rolling up a magazine tightly, taping it, wrapping it in wool or heavy cotton fabric, tucking the ends into the tube, and fastening them. Fell the closing (Fig. 14). It can also be made by cutting a rolling pin in

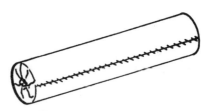

Fig. 14.   A seam roll.

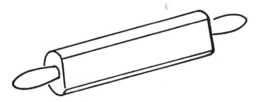

Fig. 15. A seam board.

half lengthwise, padding it, and covering it tightly (Fig. 15) — also called a seam board.

Sewing machine. A well-regulated stitching machine, cleaned and oiled, is necessary.

Shears. The shears should have a sharp point and be from 8 to 10 in. long; however, a 7-in. dressmaker's shears may be substituted.

Sheet and towel. Used for shrinking material.

*****Sleeve board.** A board shaped like a folded sleeve used for pressing seams of sleeves and darts. Sometimes they may be purchased ready made. Support A can be made from a piece of 2 by 4-in. lumber or any similar material (Fig. 16).

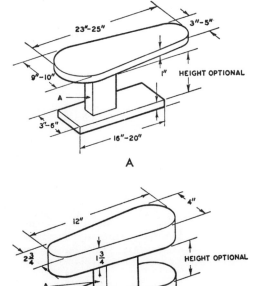

Fig. 16. Two kinds of sleeve boards: A, for sleeves; B, for sleeve caps and shoulder area.

Sleeve press pad. A stuffed pad shaped like a sleeve used for pressing sleeves. It may be purchased at a tailor's supply house.

Sponge. A cellulose or natural sponge is used to apply moisture to the press cloth for pressing.

Sponge cloth. A cloth or sheet used to shrink wool material.

Square or yardstick. A rule used to check material for grain perfection.

Stiletto. A pointed instrument used to make a hole for the eyelet of a worked buttonhole. A sharp-pointed scissors or orange stick may also be used.

Tailor's bench. The tailor uses a table from 3 to 4 ft. wide by 4 to 6 ft. long for all of his work, including cutting, pressing, etc. In the center, it may be padded to be used for pressing, or a cheese block is used.

Tailor's chalk (pipe clay). Wax chalk is used on wool, and clay chalk, which is made of pipe clay, on linings. Wax melts and stains if not used carefully.

*****Tailor's ham.** A ham-shaped, stuffed, cloth-covered object used in pressing any shaped and curved surfaces, the ends of a dart, etc. This is covered with cotton drill on one side and wool on the other side, and filled with lint cotton, sawdust, wool ravelings, or sand. Tailor's hams vary in size and shape. Some are round, about 6 in. in diameter, and about an

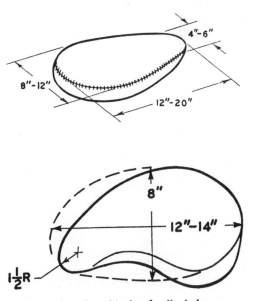

Fig. 17. Two kinds of tailor's hams.

inch thick (Fig. 18). Also called a *cushion* or *press pad*.

Tapeline. A linen, cotton, or plastic measure, with metal-tipped edges, 60 in. long and reversible. Also called a *measure*.

Thimble. A metal object worn over the third finger of the right hand. A tailor's thimble is open at the end; however, a nickel-plated dressmaker's thimble which fits well can be used effectively.

Tracing paper. Assorted colors of tracing paper are used for marking with a tracing wheel. Typewriter carbon paper should not be used.

Tracing wheel. A round, serrated, or needle-pointed wheel with a handle, used to trace markings from a pattern to the fabric.

Velvet or needle board. A board with numerous steel needles about ¼ in. in length used to press velvet and pile fabrics. As a substitute a standing iron may be covered with a wet cloth and the wrong side of the velvet drawn over a steaming iron.

Wooden cloth board. A board 6 to 12 in. wide, 32 in. long, and at least ¾ in. thick around which cloth is wound to shrink wool the "London Shrunk" method. The sharp edges should be rounded. As a substitute, a cylinder from a bolt of material may be used.

Wrist pincushion. A pincushion on a bracelet band. It may be constructed by attaching onto a small pincushion a circle or elastic to fit the wrist.

KEY

WOOL – Right Side	▭	LINING – Right Side	▥
WOOL – Wrong Side	▩	LINING – Wrong Side	▤
CANVAS	▨	SILESIA	▧
WIGAN	▨	STAY	▨
CORD, TAPE	▦	MELTON	▨

Key for the drawings.

CHAPTER 4

Selecting a Pattern

WHEN you select a style, consider your present wardrobe and your needs. Choose a style that will be suitable for the places you go and is appropriate for your figure; select a color that highlights your natural coloring and harmonizes with your present wardrobe; and use a fabric that suits the design, your figure, and will tailor well. To aid you in planning for this custom-tailored garment, use the "Wardrobe Planning Guide" on p. 159.

The suit that answers all of these needs for the average woman is often the basic suit which travels around the clock. It probably will be a soft, dressmaker type of a plain, neutral color, such as black, navy, dark brown, or gray. The fabric should be light in weight so that the suit can be worn in all seasons. If the neckline is simple, collars and scarves may be added for variety. A suit with self-covered buttons that can be worn without a blouse is still more versatile.

Here are some suggestions to make the basic suit go "round the clock":

Early morning: tailored hat; closed-toe shoes; scarf with geometric motifs; plain pearls; jet, gold, or silver jewelry; and gloves.

Casual daytime wear: casual hat and bag, blouse with matching bow, and gloves.

Luncheon: print blouse with matching hat and blending tones for gloves and bag. For more formal occasions, small hat, ascot, kidskin gloves, and perhaps a flower at the neck.

Dinner or theater: velvet hat, suede bag, chiffon scarf at the neck, and glitter in jewelry; kidskin or suede gloves may be added.

These additional suggestions may prove helpful to persons of the various body types indicated:

Short figure: smooth, soft fabric; vertical lines; semifitted jacket and full-length coats.

Thin, angular figure: napped surfaces and bulky textures; horizontal lines and widely spaced designs; shoulder accents; full skirts; full-length, semifitted coats; dolman sleeves.

Bulging middle: box jacket suit; skirt with easy fit.

Overweight figure: straight, vertical lines; plain two-piece sleeves; avoid patch pockets and any crosswise detail; easy-fitting jacket; set-in pockets placed diagonally or vertically; easy fit over bust.

Tall and heavy boned figure: lightweight fabrics — not excessively bulky, crisp, or clinging types; plain designs, such as semitailored dressmaker suits.

On pages 10 and 11 are sketches of some suit coat styles that are favorites today. Analyze yourself; choose the suit or coat best for you (Fig. 21).

Next take the following four body measurements (Fig. 22).

Bust: _____ inches — taken around the fullest part of the bust; snug, but not tight.

Waist: _____ inches — taken snugly at natural waistline.

Hip: _____ inches — taken snugly around fullest part, about 7 in. below the waistline.

Back waist length: _____ inches — taken from the prominent bone at the base of the back of the neck to the waistline.

Measurements should be taken over a smooth fitting dress or blouse and smooth

Clutch coat   Wrap-around   Walking suit

Man (hard) tailored   Blazer   Belted tailored

Fig. 21A. Coat and suit styles.

| Bolero | Chanel (box style) | Dressmaker | Man's sport coat |

Fig. 21B. Coat and suit styles.

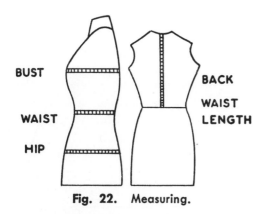

Fig. 22. Measuring.

scriptive of age, but are based on height, contour of figure, and body proportions.

When you have decided upon a figure type, select a pattern size made for that figure type from the Revised Measurement Chart," p. 14. Choose the pattern size which most nearly fits your body measurements — not ready-to-wear size or by age; however, the new sizing corresponds more closely to the sizes available in ready-to-wear.

Patterns allow for "pattern ease" and sometimes "design ease." For "pattern ease" some pattern companies allow, on a simple fitted garment, from 2 to 4½ in. in the bust, ½ in. on the waist, 2 in. on the hip, and ¼ in. on the waist length.

Pattern ease or "tolerance" also varies according to figure type and somewhat between pattern designers. For example, one company allows the following:

fitting slip or skirt. You should be wearing a bra and proper foundation garment. Use a firm tape measure.

Record the measurements on the "Personal and Pattern Measurement Chart," p. 12 (A: 1, 2, 3, and 4).

After taking your measurements, determine your figure type from Figure 23. *Remember:* The figure types are not de-

Bust: 3-in. ease on Misses, Junior, Junior Petite, Young Junior/Teen Sizes. 4-in. ease on Half-Sizes. 4½-in. ease on Women's Sizes.

Waist: 1-in. ease on all patterns.

Hips: 2½-in. ease on Misses, Half-Size, Junior Petite, Junior Sizes. 3-in. ease on Women's Sizes.

Back waist length: ⅛-in. ease on all pattern sizes.

Another company allows 1¼ in. more ease for a jacket than a dress (4¼-in. ease), and 1¼ in. more for a coat than a jacket (5¼-in. ease).

Pattern types "Misses," "Women's," "Half Size," "Junior," and "Junior Petite," are designed for the fully developed figure.

Misses' patterns are designed for a well-proportioned figure. About 5'5"–5'6" without shoes.

Junior Petite patterns are designed for a well-proportioned petite figure. About 5'–5'1" without shoes.

Junior patterns are designed for a well-proportioned shorter waisted figure. About 5'4"–5'5" without shoes.

Women's patterns are designed for the larger more fully mature figure. About 5'5"–5'6" without shoes.

Half-size patterns are for a fully developed figure with a short backwaist length. Waist and hip are larger in proportion to bust than other figure types. About 5'2"–5'3" without shoes.

New Size Range. The Young Junior/Teen category is designed primarily for Junior-Hi girls who have outgrown the 7–14 size range. In fashion and fit, this new size range is created for the developing pre-teen and teen figures. About 5'1"–5'3" without shoes.

Fig. 23.   Pattern types.

In addition, some patterns have "design ease," such as shirring, gathering, tucks, blouson effect, and pleats to provide additional ease allowance.

Because of the bustline "pattern ease" allowance, some persons who measure slightly larger than the pattern may not need to select a larger size since they may not desire the full amount of 2 in. to 4½ in. ease in their garment. Likewise, in an A-line or full skirt, one may not need to add extra in the hip because of "design ease" plus the 1½ in. to 2 in. "pattern ease."

If you are choosing a blouse, suit, or coat pattern, your bust measurement will determine the size you need. The patterns allow adequate ease. If you are purchasing a separate skirt pattern, your waist and hip measurement will determine the size. Select a straight skirt pattern by hip measurement. If the skirt is full, one may buy the pattern according to the waistline measure.

If your measurements are not exactly the same as any in the chart, choose the size closest depending on the pattern and design ease and whether you wear your clothes snugger or looser. Choose the pattern size which more closely fits the shoulder area as alterations in that area are apt to be more difficult to make.

BODY MEASUREMENTS — NEW SIZING

| | MISSES' | | | | | | |
| | About 5'5"–5'6" Without Shoes | | | | | | |
Buy Size	6	8	10	12	14	16	18
If Bust is	30½	31½	32½	34	36	38	40
Waist	22	23	24	25½	27	29	31
Hip	32½	33½	34½	36	38	40	42
Back Waist Length	15½	15¾	16	16¼	16½	16¾	17

| | WOMEN'S | | | | | | |
| | About 5'5"–5'6" Without Shoes | | | | | | |
Buy Size	38	40	42	44	46	48	50
If Bust is	42	44	46	48	50	52	54
Waist	34	36	38	40½	43	45½	48
Hip	44	46	48	50	52	54	56
Back Waist Length	17¼	17⅜	17½	17⅝	17¾	17⅞	18

JUNIOR
About 5'4"–5'5" Without Shoes

Buy Size	5	7	9	11	13	15
If Bust is	30	31	32	33½	35	37
Waist	21½	22½	23½	24½	26	28
Hip	32	33	34	35½	37	39
Back Waist Length	15	15¼	15½	15¾	16	16¼

HALF
About 5'2"–5'3" Without Shoes

Buy Size	10	12	14	16	18	20	22	24
If Bust is	33	35	37	39	41	43	45	47
Waist	26	28	30	32	34	36½	39	41½
Hip	35	37	39	41	43	45½	48	50½
Back Waist Length	15	15¼	15½	15¾	15⅞	16	16⅛	16¼

JUNIOR PETITE
About 5'–5'1" Without Shoes

Buy Size	3JP	5JP	7JP	9JP	11JP	13JP
If Bust is	30½	31	32	33	34	35
Waist	22	22½	23½	24½	25½	26½
Hip	31½	32	33	34	35	36
Back Waist Length	14	14¼	14½	14¾	15	15¼

YOUNG JUNIOR/TEEN —
NEW SIZE RANGE
About 5'1"–5'3" Without Shoes

Buy Size	5/6	7/8	9/10	11/12	13/14	15/16
If Bust is	28	29	30½	32	33½	35
Waist	22	23	24	25	26	27
Hip	31	32	33½	35	36½	38
Back Waist Length	13½	14	14½	15	15⅜	15¾

SKIRTS, SLACKS AND SHORTS
Misses'

Waist	22	23	24	25½	27	29	31 Ins.
Hip	32½	33½	34½	36	38	40	42 Ins.

Women's

Waist	34	36	38	40½	43	45½	48 Ins.
Hip	44	46	48	50	52	54	56 Ins.

Young Junior/Teen

Waist	22	23	24	25	26 Ins.
Hip	31	32	33½	35	36½ Ins.

Junior

Waist	21½	22½	23½	24½	26	28 Ins.
Hip	32	33	34	35½	37	39 Ins.

Junior Petite

Waist	22	22½	23½	24½	25½	26½ Ins.
Hip	31½	32	33	34	35	36 Ins.

MENS

Size (Chest)	32	34	36	38	40	42	44	46	48	50
Waist	28	30	32	34	36	38	40	42	44	46
Neck band	13½	14	14½	15	15½	16	16½	17	17½	18
Shirt sleeve length	33	33	33	33	34	34	34	35	35	35

BOYS

Buy Size	1	2	3	4	5	6	8	10	12	14	16
If Chest is	20	21	22	23	23½	24	26	28	30	32	34
Waist	19½	20	20½	21	21½	22	23	24	25½	27	29
Hip	—	—	—	—	24	25	27	29	31	33	35
Neck band	—	—	—	—	—	11½	12	12½	13	13½	14
Shirt sleeve length	—	17	18	19	20	21	23	25	27	29	(Not stated)

NOTE:

1. Vogue does not offer Mens and Boys patterns. All other pattern types are available from Butterick, McCalls, Simplicity, and Vogue Pattern Companies.

2. Most of the size ranges within the different pattern figures types have been extended to correspond more closely to the size available in ready-to-wear. The size ranges are as follows:

Misses'	6–18	Half Size	10–24	Junior	5–15
Women's	38–50	Junior Petite	3–13	Young Junior/Teen	⅝–¹⅝₁₆

A design is not always available in every size within a category, nor are all categories offered by each pattern company.

3. Patterns purchased through newspapers and magazines may not conform to the measurement standards of the pattern industry.

PERSONAL AND PATTERN MEASUREMENT CHART
My Measurement + Ease (Pattern and Design) = Pattern + Alteration

Measurements	Pattern-Size Measurement	Pattern Ease	My Measurement	Measurement of Pattern	Amount to Alter Pattern + or — in Inches
A. General Measurements 1. Bust		2″–4½″ suits 4½″–6″ coats			
2. Waist		¾–1″ skirt ½″–1″ dress			
3. Hip		1½″–2″			
4. Back waist length		0–½″			
B. Blouse 1. Base of neck at back to point of bust.		0			
2. Base of neck at center back, over high point of bust to waist.		0–½″			
3. Front chest width 6″ below shoulder at neck.		¼″–½″			

Personal and Pattern Measurement Chart (Cont.)

4. Base of neck at back to waistline.	½"			
5. Back shoulder width 4" below bone at back of neck.	½"–1"			
6. Base of neck at back to point of shoulder.	0			
7. a) Shoulder at neck over point of bust to waistline. b) Shoulder at tip to waistline.	0–½"			
C. Sleeve 1. Base of neck at back to elbow (bend elbow).	0			
2. Base of neck at back to wrist (bend elbow).	0			
3. From elbow to wrist.	0			
4. Around upper arm at fullest part.	3"			
5. Around wrist at wristbone.	½"–1" dress ½"–2" on suit			
D. Skirt and Coat Length 1. From waist to hem at center front and center back.	3" hem			
2. From back of neck at back, to hem (floor for evening coat).	1½"–3" hem			

Note:

1. The tailor's method of checking patterns uses the prominent bone at the base of the neck as a measuring aid.

2. Pattern ease refers to the allowance added to a basic pattern; whereas, design ease indicates an additional allowance for tucks, gathers, and "bloused effect."

3. Chalk-mark on the body approximately 3 in. from the prominent bone at the back of the neck to establish the shoulder seamline. Also, mark the shoulder point at the tip of the shoulder to facilitate measuring. This is especially helpful when measuring B, 7 (a) and (b), in the above chart.

4. After completing the pattern and body measurements, compute your pattern alterations according to the formula at the beginning of the above chart.

CHAPTER 5

Selecting Material, Lining, Interfacings, Underlining, Interlining, and Trimmings

Selecting Material

BECAUSE tailoring requires accurate fitting, precision stitching, molding, and pressing, it is important that the material be of good quality. Generally speaking, an all-wool fabric more nearly meets the demands for good tailoring. However, some of the new synthetic and wool blends are satisfactory, provided the proportion of blend is correct for the style of the garment and the amount of molding to be done.

"Cloths" of wool are usually sold in 54 to 60-in. widths and are folded lengthwise. The right sides of the material are folded to the inside. It is wise to note whether the cloth has correct grain alignment on the bolt.

The fabrics that yield well to tailoring are medium in thickness, spongy, have an unfinished or "nappy" surface, and are of simple construction, such as a twill weave. A soft yarn molds well, but care must be taken that it is not so soft that the finished garment will fail to hold a press and become "baggy." The "nappy" fabric does not stretch or fray as readily as some smooth "cloths." Unfinished fabrics, such as tweeds, are easy to work because they shape easily and crooked seams are not so apparent. For tailoring women's suits, 12- to 13-oz. cloth is desirable. The trend now is toward lighter weight fabrics. Last, a high-grade wool should feel resilient and "alive."

Some "cloths" which are difficult to handle in tailoring are firm, hard-finished yarns, unnapped surfaces, and very firm weaves. Fabrics which fall into these categories are coverts, sheens, and gabardines. The latter can be shrunk little, are difficult to press without shine, leave press marks, and show seam edges. Tweeds of very loose weave and dress weight fabrics are often unsatisfactory.

Another fabric which is difficult for the beginner to handle is heavy coating, such as camel's hair, the grainline of which is difficult to follow. For this reason one layer of fabric may slip in long seams. This fabric is difficult to press because the nap mats, and lapel and collar edges are bulky.

Plaids, stripes, and checks require more material because the fabric must be matched at the seams. Plaids and stripes require more planning time, but are often a rewarding challenge to the advanced student of tailoring.

When choosing the color of your fabric, consider your own personal coloring, your body type, and the needs of your present wardrobe. Remember that lighter colors make you look larger, and dark colors tend to make you look smaller.

A soft-textured fabric would be a good choice for a short, stout figure; a tall, well-proportioned person could choose tweeds, plaids, and heavier textures.

Buy the amount of material suggested

on the pattern envelope for the pattern size selected and the width of the fabric. If you choose a plaid, striped, or a napped fabric, you must allow extra material. In this case use the yardage suggested for a "fabric with nap."

Selecting Lining

The lining is almost as important as the wool fabric because it receives a great deal of hard wear. The lining fabric should be durable, opaque, colorfast to perspiration, capable of being dry cleaned, should harmonize in color with the suit fabric, and be smooth so that one can put on the garment easily.

For dressy coats and suits made of expensive materials, a pure dye silk fabric could be used for the lining. These come in heavy crepe, satin, or taffeta, and wear reasonably well.

Rayon is the most commonly used lining material. It can be purchased in crepes, satins, serge, twill weave, crepe-back satin (plain), Jacquard weave pattern, or a taffeta.

For the "custom look," the suit jacket or coat may be lined with a print, and a blouse made of the same material.

Wool linings, plaid or plain, or quilted linings are used for heavy coats. Sometimes napped cotton is used for lining, backed by a wool interlining. In coats, the shoulder area may be wool lined, and the rest lined in napped cotton.

Lining fabric woven or laminated to the interlining is available. It saves time and bulk when tailoring winter coats. (See "Interlining.")

Another type of lining is weather insulated. This is a crepe, twill, or satin fabric backed with a coating of aluminum. The purpose of this metal-insulated lining is to make the garment an "all season" one. After many dry cleanings, it may lose some of the insulating properties.

Selecting Interfacings

Interfacing is a material used between the outer cloth and its facing. Collars, cuffs, front openings, hems of jackets and coats, tabs, welts and flaps, necklines, waistbands, and buttonholes are interfaced. The interfacing should be compatible in weight and "hand" to the cloth.

Hair canvas (containing rayon, polyester, cotton, wool, and goat hair) in the appropriate weight is a suitable interfacing for most tailored wool garments. Armo P20 is used for heavy coats and suits; Armo P17, Armo Fino, and Sta-Shape SS77 are suitable for medium weight wools; and Armo P27 for lightweight coats and suits. All hair canvas is dry cleanable.

For washable coats and suits where shaping is desired, Armo Acro is a suitable choice of interfacing. Formite, Sta-Shape (SS65) may also be used.

For lightweight suits of raw silk, silk shantung, etc., one may use Sta-Shape SS50 which is washable and dry cleanable. Super Siri (comes in three weights) and Veriform, both of 100% rayon, are both lightweight and washable or dry cleanable.

Nonwoven interfacing (Interlon, Pellon and Keyback) do not have the drapeability of woven interfacings. They are best used for crisp shaping. They are washable and dry cleanable. Bias Pellon is lightweight and gives in all directions.

Press-on interfacings are available in both woven and nonwoven fabrics. They are applied with heat and a press cloth. One must be sure that the outer fabric can withstand the heat needed for application and that they do not show a "line" on the outer garment. They become firmer and stiffer when bonded to the fabric. These are best for crisp effects for small areas.

Some brands of woven press-on interfacings are Armo P92, P91, Red Edge and Fino, Facemate, and Staflex All Purpose and Staflex for Wools. Nonwoven press-on interfacings are: Staflex Non Woven, Pelomite (Detail and Shape Retaining), and Keybak Hot Iron.

Selecting Interlining

Winter coats for cold climates are often interlined with a separate fabric. Chamois, lamb's wool (often quilted), outing flannel, or a coarsely woven lightweight wool fabric interlining may be used. A lining-interlining can be purchased with a rayon-satin top backed by fleeced cotton, wool and cotton combination, or napped dacron. A recent lining-interlining combination is a urethane foam which is laminated to rayon or acetate fabric. Sometimes interlinings are made detachable so the garment can be worn during different seasons of the year.

A pile fabric with a knitted backing is available in 14 colors, 60 in. wide. It may be used as lining and interlining and is called Carmolon 1000. It is washable and dry cleanable.

Dorron, 100% wool, 48 in. wide, available in black and white, is an interlining for coats and jackets and a backing for quilting. It is hand washable or dry cleanable.

Earl-Glo De-Luxe is a satin acetate lining with a foam backing. It is a lining and interlining as is Sunbak satin with an acrylic napped backing. Both are dry cleanable.

Milium Plus is an insulated lining with a foam interlining laminated.

Warmo is a 100% wool insulation interlining in a 54 in. width.

Selecting Underlining

Underlinings give support and shape to the fabric, prevent sagging and stretching, add crease resistance, and create fashion detail effects. The garment and underlining are treated as one during construction. To eliminate bulk, the darts or tucks may be sewn separately before stay-stitching the two together.

Slim skirts made of lightweight wool or crepe and A-line skirts are usually underlined with a firmly woven fabric, but not heavier than the garment fabric. Voile, organza, soft lightweight taffeta sheath lining, China silk, or a commercial underlining are suitable.

Suit jackets and coats of gauzy wool, knit, or jersey may be underlined with a matching color in lightweight cotton, silk organza, or a commercial underlining as sheath or Si Bonne. The darts may be treated separately or as one, depending on the effect desired. The garment is then lined.

Cotton sheath underlining is available in a variety of colors, is lightweight, 2% shrinkage controlled, and is washable and dry cleanable. It is excellent for lightweight and naked wools.

An acetate underlining is Eternachrome, which is soft, lightweight, washable, and dry cleanable. It is perspiration proof, will not fade, and is 45 in. wide.

Living-lining is a lightweight rayon underlining for stretch fabrics with 30% minimum stretch. It, too, is washable and dry cleanable.

Sheer De Swa is a 100% cotton batiste available in a variety of colors. It is excellent for wash and wear suits, light fabrics, and children's clothes.

Si Bonne, a 100% rayon of Avron and Bemberg, is available in black and white and 48 colors. It comes in soft and crisp textures. It is dry cleanable, but may be washed. It may be used for underlining lightweight wools, raw silks, and blends.

A sheath of 100% acetate, available in black and white and about 65 colors, is the most common underlining used. It is washable or dry cleanable and is 39 in. wide.

Taffeta, Touché (100% rayon), China silk (habutae — Japanese name for China silk), silk organza, or voile are other lightweight underliners. The Veriform basic liner (70% rayon and 30% cotton, 39 in. wide), available in black, white, and natural, is excellent for dress weight suits. Muslins and lightweight percales may also be used for underlining coats and jackets.

Selecting Trimmings (Findings)

In addition to the wool fabric and the lining, other supplies known as "trimming" or "findings" are required to tailor the garment. The tailor may call them "trimmings."

Binding. May be bias or straight. It is one method used for finishing skirt seams, skirt hems, unlined jacket seams, and men's sport-coat seams. The binding may be of rayon or silk, and should match the wool in color.

Buttons. Should be durable and dry cleanable. Self-covered buttons of matching fabric can be used or uncovered buttons can be purchased. For a man's garment buy size No. 30 for the coat front and No. 24 for the sleeves.

Buttonhole twist. This silk twist should be matched to the fabric and is used for hand-worked buttonholes.

Canvas. A constructed canvas can be purchased from a tailor for a man's sport coat or one can be made. See Chapter 11.

Cotton felt and wadding. Used for shaping around the armscye, at the top half of the sleeve seam and to construct shoulder pads.

Gimp. A heavy thread used to pad tailored worked buttonholes.

Haircloth (optional). Used to make canvas for a man's sport coat.

Interfacing (reinforcement). Hymo (a canvas with or without hair) used to reinforce the body of the coat front.

Hook and eye. A fastener often used at the end of the skirt belt.

Linen canvas. Used to reinforce the collar of a man's coat or for hard tailoring.

Shoulder pads. Ready-made shoulder pads are available in practically any style and weight. Cotton or wool batting or sheet wadding may be used to make them. They are covered with muslin or wigan.

Silesia or pocketing. Should be near the hue of the garment. It is used for men's, children's garments, or coats since it wears better than lining.

Skirt lining. A firm material as taffeta or lining material is used to line the back or the front and back of the skirt, especially straight skirts and those of loosely woven materials. Crepe or satin may be used for lightweight wools. The color of the lining should not show through the wool.

Sleeve head. A stitched sheet wadding used at sleeve-armscye seams. It may be purchased ready made at a tailor's supply house.

Stay tape. Preferably this should be linen, ⅜ in. wide for staying creaseline, lapel, front edges, and lower armscye seams. Twill tape or selvage can be used as a substitute.

Thread. Choose silk thread of matching color or a shade darker than the wool. A matching heavy-duty or hand-sewing silk is often used for sewing on buttons, bar tacks, and putting in linings. Silk buttonhole twist can also be used for buttons. Sometimes heavy-duty thread is used for stitching armscye seams and underarm seams where there may be strain. Subsilk is a tailor's substitute for silk thread. It is available for the home sewer at the supply houses listed on p. 161.

Underlining. A lightweight lining cut like the garment and sewed into the seams. The garment and lining are treated as one. This gives the cloth support and shape to the garment. A suit jacket, skirt, or a complete coat may be underlined.

Undercollar fabric. Melton or firm flannel may be used for hard-tailored garments.

Wigan. Used for body back interfacing, hem interfacings, pocket stays, interfacing for turned-back cuffs, and buttonhole reinforcement. Some tailors use linen for stays; muslin may also be substituted. Wigan is available in 2½ in. width bias strips for sleeve and hem interfacing and by the yard for back interfacing.

Zipper. The slide fastener should match the wool fabric in color, and be 6 or 7 in. in length. The size should be in harmony with the weight of the fabric.

CHAPTER 6

Preparing Material, Lining, Trimmings, and Interfacings

Preparing the Material

Fabrics used for tailoring must be preshrunk before use. This is a relaxation shrinkage which eliminates the dimensional change in the cloth which occurred during the manufacturing process. Many woolen cloths are preshrunk by the manufacturer and are labeled "London Shrunk," "Mill Shrunk," "Preshrunk," or "Ready for the Needle." Sometimes, however, wool is only partly shrunk by this method, so it may be desirable to test the fabric, and if need be, preshrink it before sewing. Secondly, a fabric that has been factory preshrunk may need to be treated again to return the fabric to grain perfection.

To test the fabric, place a dampened press cloth over the fabric in one corner, and press with a iron set at the marking "Wool" (350° F.–375° F.) and hold the iron in position while counting from one to seven. Remove the iron and press cloth. If there are no iron markings or wrinkles on the fabric, there is no need to shrink the fabric further. If there are, it would be better to preshrink so the fabric will be dimensionally stable and will not shrink during the construction steam pressing or from atmospheric conditions, body moisture, or subsequent dry cleaning.

Another method for testing fabric for shrinkage is to cut a 6 in. square of fabric. Steam press, then measure after pressing.

If gauzy woolens and mohairs are preshrunk, the fabric may lose the "open" quality and texture. These fabrics are usually underlined to keep them stable. Some fabrics may lose their "finish" also by preshrinking. It is then a matter of choice for the home sewer if she prefers to preshrink these fabrics and perhaps lose some of the above mentioned qualities in order to insure dimensional stability.

Some other fabrics used for coats and suits which present special problems in preparing them for cutting are:

Foam-backed fabric. No preparation needed but choose a fabric that is laminated on grain.

Stretch. Check the label on the bolt and if the percentage of shrinkage is more than 2%, press with a steam iron before cutting.

Double knits. Shrink by steam pressing or London Shrunk method unless the label indicates this has been done. Run a thread along a rib line for the grain.

Jersey. If not labeled against shrinkage, preshrink by washing if constructing a washable garment or steam press or London Shrink if it is to be dry cleaned. "Tebilized," "Redmanized," and "Pak-nit" are trade name guarantees of shrinkage control.

Corduroys and Velvets. Steam press on a needleboard to remove wrinkles.

Cottons and Linens. Preshrink by immersion in water unless guaranteed less than 1 to 2% shrinkage. (See Preparing the Lining.) If the material is preshrunk and slightly off-grain, steam press it to restore the grain.

Silk. Shrink using a steam iron.

Synthetics (Wash and Wear). Need not be preshrunk, but may be steam pressed to straighten the grain. Blends containing over 65% synthetic fibers will not shrink appreciably.

Deep pile fabrics. Check the label regarding shrinkage. Many backings are stabilized and some which are not shrink excessively. If not labeled, test a measured piece if you desire to wash the finished garment.

Retailers, tailoring establishments, or dry-cleaning houses often offer preshrinking service. It is not difficult to shrink fabric yourself. The methods described in this chapter are all acceptable for shrinking fabrics at home.

Method I. London Shrunk

MATERIALS NEEDED: sponge cloth — sheet folded in half lengthwise; wooden cloth board (see Chapter 3, p. 8)

1. Straighten the cut ends.
A. Tear or pull a thread or baste a line along a crosswise thread.
B. Cut along the straight grain if a thread is pulled.

II. Fold the fabric lengthwise and baste the ends together.
A. Baste-stitch by machine or hand-baste the cut ends together by matching the edges or the line of basting.
B. Often the selvages are basted also.

III. Place the cloth on the table.
Place the folded edge away from you.

IV. Measure the cloth.
A. Measure the length and width of the material.
B. Write down the measurements.

V. Snip the selvages (optional).
A. Clip the selvages at 2- to 3-in. intervals along the edge; or
B. Cut off the selvages.

VI. Saturate the sponge cloth in warm water.
A. Soak the sponge cloth thoroughly so there are no dry spots on it.
B. Wring out the excess water.

VII. Lay the wool cloth on the wet sponge cloth.
A. Spread the wool cloth smoothly over the sponge cloth.
B. Be sure the sponge cloth is smooth, too, because wrinkles are difficult to remove from the wool cloth.

VIII. Roll over a wooden cloth board or cardboard tube.
A. Roll the wool cloth and the sponge cloth smoothly over and over the wooden cloth board or cardboard tube:
B. They should not be so tight that the material cannot shrink, yet no wrinkles should be produced.

IX. Cover the roll with a Turkish towel, plastic, or a newspaper to retain moisture and lay it aside to dampen.
A. Lightweight wool dampens thoroughly in 2 hours, but heavy fabrics may require even 12 hours. Most authorities recommend 4 to 8 hours or even overnight.
B. Some tailors allow this material to dry almost completely on the roll.

X. Unroll the cloth and remove the sponge cloth.
Observe that the wool is completely dampened.

XI. Dry the material.
A. Smooth the material gently.
B. Check the grain lines on a flat surface (Fig. 25).

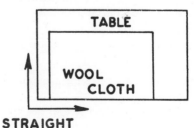

STRAIGHT

Fig. 25. Checking the grain lines.

C. Dry the material flat on the table or on the floor. The cloth may also be hung over a shower rod or padded door and shifted from time to time as it is drying.

D. Pressing is unnecessary; however, some tailors recommend a little pressing.

Method II. London Shrunk Method (Without Board)

I–VI. Same as Method I.

VII. Lay the wool material on the wet sponge cloth.

A. Place the wool material on the center of the sheet (Fig. 26).

B. Fold the edges of the sheet over the ends and sides of the fabric (Fig. 26).

C. Beginning at one end, roll loosely into a cylinder (Fig. 26).

VIII. Cover, roll, and lay aside the material.

IX–XI. Same as Method I.

Method III. Shrinking by Pressing

I. Fold the fabric lengthwise, basting together the selvages and the straightened ends.

II. Shrink the material by pressing (see Chapter 8, p. 39).

A. Place a dry wool cloth next to the wool, and a damp cloth on top of this. The top cloth may be moistened with a wet sponge. (Another dry cloth may be used on top to protect your hand.)

B. Press flat on both sides.   ·

C. Begin at the selvage and press toward the fold but do not press a crease in the folded area.

III. Remove the bastings and open the material.

A. Press the unpressed center lengthwise on the wrong side.

B. Press out the imprints of bastings if there are any.

C. Do not press completely dry.

IV. Dry the material.

A. Spread the material flat to dry.

LAY WOOL ON WET SHEET

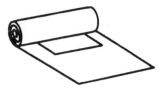

ROLL INTO CYLINDER

Fig. 26.   London shrinking.

B. If no space is available for drying the material flat, hang it over a round rod, being sure that it is straight. Shift its position while drying so that its own weight will not stretch it.

Sometimes if the torn or drawn ends are very uneven, it may be necessary to mark the filling threads and the warp lines about every 18 in. Match these and shrink out the puffiness between the markings. Match the lines of a plaid in the same manner.

Preparing the Lining

Most rayon and silk linings need only be pressed to be smoothed before cutting. Often crepe lining has to be steam-pressed well, because it may shrink during the dry cleaning and pressing of the garment. If you anticipate excessive shrinkage, the material should be shrunk in the following manner:

I. Soak the cloth in cool water.
A. Baste together the straightened ends and the selvages; fold the cloth and place it in water.
B. Squeeze out the excess water. Do not wring.

II. Remove the excess water.
Roll the cloth in a Turkish towel and press out the excess water.

III. Hang the cloth to dry, or dry it on a smooth, flat surface.
A. Smooth the selvages and ends.
B. Hang the cloth on a rod and let the remainder of the water evaporate.
C. Dry it until damp.

IV. Press the cloth.
A. Place the cloth straight on the ironing board.
B. Set the iron at the correct temperature for the fabric.
C. Press on the wrong side, with the grain.

Preparing the Interlining

Wool and cotton interlinings may be steam pressed to shrink.

Preparing the Trimmings

The trimmings or findings should be properly prepared for use, to prevent shrinkage during dry cleaning and steam pressing. This would cause puckers and ruin the appearance of the garment.

Stay tape, grosgrain belting, rayon and silk seam tape, and cotton tape are shrunk in the following manner:

I. Place the tape in warm water.
A. Either remove the tape from the roll or break the cardboard and leave the tape on the roll or container.
B. Place it in water so that the tape is completely soaked.

II. Remove the excess water.
A. Blot out the water by rolling the tape in a Turkish towel.
B. If the tape is left on the roll, allow it to dry on the roll; no pressing is necessary.

III. Press the tape if it has been removed from the roll.
Press it in a lengthwise direction, keeping the edges straight.

Preparing the Interfacings

Muslin, wigan, and tailor's canvas are also prepared before tailoring a garment.

I. Soak the cloth in lukewarm water.
This should be done for about twenty minutes.

II. Remove the excess water.
Squeeze or press out the excess water in a towel.

III. Hang the cloth to dry.
A. Hang the cloth smooth and straight on a rod.
B. Dry it until it is only damp.

IV. Press the cloth.
Press it smooth while it is still damp.

CHAPTER 7

Fitting a Pattern

YOU have selected a pattern that most nearly resembles your measurements, and you are now ready to check the fit of your pattern.

First of all, select the view from the envelope which you are planning to make. Remove all the pattern pieces from the envelope. If you are in a class, it is a good idea to write your name on each. If the pattern is wrinkled, press the pieces you will use with a warm iron. The parts you will not need can be returned to the envelope.

Take your body measurements and record them on the "Personal and Pattern Measurement Chart" (pp. 12–13). Remember:

1. Use a firm accurate tape measure.
2. Take measurements over a good-fitting bra, foundation garment, and smooth-fitting garment or slip.
3. Take measurements accurately, but not too tight.

Taking Personal Measurements

I. Take the general measurements.

A. Place the tape measure snugly around the bust at the fullest part (Fig. 29, A).

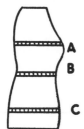

Fig. 29. General measurements.

B. Place the tape measure around the natural waistline snugly, but not too tight (Fig. 29, B).
C. Measure down 7 in. from the natural waistline, or lower if the fullest part of the hip is lower (Fig. 29, C).

II. Take the blouse measurements.

A. Measure from the prominent bone at the back of the neck along the basic neckline to the point of the bust (Fig. 30, A).

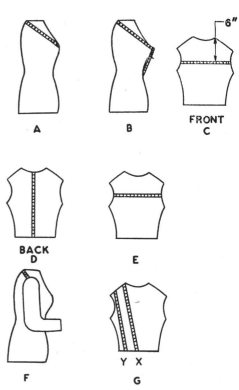

Fig. 30. Blouse measurements.

24

B. Measure from the prominent bone at the back of the neck following the curve over the point of the bust, to the natural waistline below the point of the bust (Fig. 30, B).

C. Measure the front chest width from armhole to armhole beginning 6 in. below the shoulder at the neck (Fig. 30, C).

D. Measure from the prominent bone at the back of the neck to the waistline (Fig. 30, D).

E. Measure down 4 in. from the prominent bone at the back of the neck and measure across the blouse back (Fig. 30, E).

F. Measure straight from the prominent bone at the back of the neck to the tip of the shoulder (Fig. 30, F).

G. 1. Measure from the shoulder line at the base of the neck over the high point of the bust to the waistline (Fig. 30, G, x).

   2. Measure from the shoulder tip straight down to the waistline. This will aid in determining the shoulder slope (Fig. 30, G, y).

III. Take the sleeve measurements.

A. Bend the elbow. Measure from the prominent bone at the back of the neck, bringing the tape measure across the tip of the shoulder, down the arm to the elbow (Fig. 31, A–B).

B. Repeat step A except continue down to the wrist (Fig. 31, A–C).

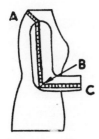

Fig. 31. Sleeve measurements.

C. Measure from the point of the elbow to the wristbone (Fig. 31, B–C).

D. Measure around the upper arm at the pit of the arm or at the fullest part of the arm.

E. Measure around the wrist over the wristbone.

IV. Measure the length of the skirt and coat.

A. Measure from the waistline to the hem at the center front and back (Fig. 32, A).

B. Measure from the prominent bone at the back of the neck to the hemline, holding the measure in at the waistline (hold the measure to the floor for a full length formal coat) (Fig. 32, B).

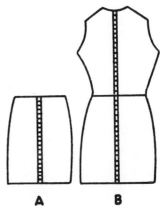

A   B

Fig. 32. Skirt and coat measurements.

Taking Pattern Measurements

Next, you are prepared to measure you pattern and record those measurements on the "Personal and Pattern Measurement Chart." Remember these points:

I. Pin the pattern together.

A. Pin in the darts at the front and the back shoulder. Pin all other darts, tucks, and pleats (Fig. 33).

B. Lap and pin the front and back

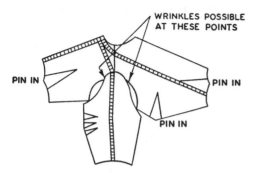

Fig. 33.   Pattern measurements.

pieces together at the shoulder seam on the stitching line (Fig. 33).

C. Match the stitching line on the top of the sleeve to the stitching line at the top of the armhole at the marking. Pin the sleeve at the underarm seam as indicated. The pattern will lie in folds at the top of the sleeve (Fig. 33).

D. Lap and pin the skirt pieces together on the stitching line.

II. Measure from the seamline of the pattern, not the cutting line.

III. Double the pattern measurements when measuring half patterns.

IV. For figures with large hips, bust, or abdomen, it may be helpful to measure the front and the back of the

KEY TO ALTERATIONS

────────────────────

POSITION OF ORIGINAL PATTERN PIECE

— — — — — — — — — —

CUTTING LINE
- - - - - - - - - - - - -
NEW POSITION

ADDITION TO PATTERN PIECE

LAP OF PATTERN PIECE

bust, hips, and waist separately, measuring from side seam to side seam. NOTE: Many methods are used for fitting and testing patterns. Some people pin the pattern together completely and try it on. Others make a complete test garment of muslin. The muslin is fitted to the individual and the original pattern adjusted accordingly. The latter method is suggested for people who have complicated fitting problems.

Pattern Alterations

In making pattern alterations, remember the following:

I. Keep the straight-of-goods in the position indicated on the pattern. Move darts or tucks to new positions, keeping the width the same until fitting.

II. Slash the pattern deep enough so that the tissue lies smooth at the pivot point.

III. Place tissue under the pattern piece when the pattern is enlarged. Use pins or cellophane tape to fasten it in position.

IV. Do not change the shape of the neckline, armholes, or shoulders any more than necessary. Try not to change the outline of your pattern. When making alterations, move the pattern piece and use it as a guide for cutting.

V. When a wedge-shaped spread is used in an area for added fullness, it often gives extra fullness in other places which may be folded out.

NOTE: The alterations most frequently needed are shown below. Others may be found in dressmaking books or booklets designated especially for pattern alterations.

Blouse Alterations

I. Shoulder alterations:

A. *For wider shoulders:* Make an L-shaped slash on the front waist and back from the center of the shoulder to about ⅛ in. from the armhole notch. Spread the slash and relocate the shoulder line from the neckline edge to the top of the armhole (Fig. 34).

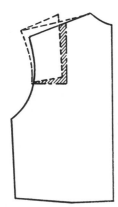

Fig. 34.   For wider shoulders.

B. *For narrower shoulders:* Slash the pattern as above and lap it to remove the desired width. Relocate the shoulder seam from the neckline edge to the top of the armhole (Fig. 35).

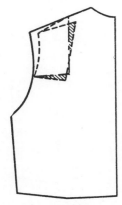

Fig. 35.   For narrower shoulders.

C. *For square shoulders:* Add to the shoulder tip by tapering from the neckline edge. Add to the underarm seam to compensate (Fig. 36).

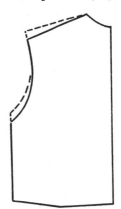

Fig. 36.   For square shoulders.

D. *For sloping shoulders:* Remove part of the shoulder seam at the outer tip of the shoulder, tapering from the neckline. Also remove the corresponding amount from the underarm seam by using the pattern as a guide in order to retain the original shape of the armhole (Fig. 37).

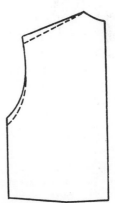

Fig. 37.   For sloping shoulders.

II. Bust alterations.

A. *For a larger bust:* Starting midway along the waistline dart, slash almost to the shoulder. Cut the pattern horizontally through the bustline dart since a large bust usually causes the pattern to be too short. Make a new underarm dart and new waistline darts. Restore the waistline measure by adding or increasing the size of the waistline darts (Fig. 38).

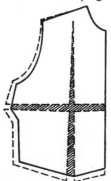

Fig. 38 For a larger bust.

B. *For a smaller bust:* Alter in the same area where additional allowance was provided for a large bust except for the horizontal line which extends to the vertical line. The side seam may need to be relocated and an extension added to the lower side section (Fig. 39).

Fig. 39. For a smaller bust.

C. *For a wider chest and bust:* Slash the pattern from 1 to 2 in. below the armscye to the point of the bust and up through the shoulder seam as indicated. Spread the pattern the desired amount and relocate the side seam (Fig. 40).

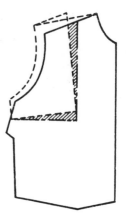

Fig. 40. For a wider chest and bust.

D. *For a narrower chest and bust:* Slash the pattern as above, but lap the edges to remove fullness (Fig. 41).

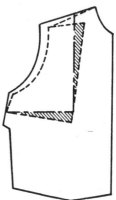

Fig. 41. For a narrower chest and bust.

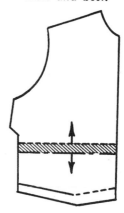

TUCK
Fig. 42. To shorten a blouse.

III. Length alterations.

A. *To shorten a blouse:* Take a tuck across the pattern in the area indicated to shorten the blouse the desired amount (Fig. 42).

B. *To lengthen a blouse:* Slash the pattern across from the center to the side seam, and spread it to add the desired amount. Keep the lengthwise grain marking in alignment (Fig. 43).

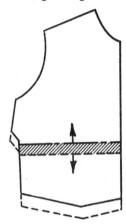

Fig. 43.   To lengthen a blouse.

IV. For a round, full back.

Slash the pattern tissue lengthwise from the waistline almost through the center of the shoulder. Slash from the center of the back to the lengthwise cut at a point 4 to 5 in.

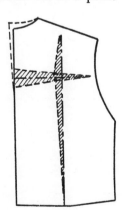

Fig. 44.   For a round, full back.

down from the center of the back neckline. Spread both slashes to give the desired amount at the widest part of the back. Keep the edges of the tissue together at the shoulder and at the waistline. Relocate the center of the back and the neckline. Several neckline darts may be needed (Fig. 44).

V. Waistline alterations.

A. *To make a blouse waist smaller:* Take a tuck near the dart or decrease at the seam. If the decrease is over ¼ in., make two darts (Fig. 45).

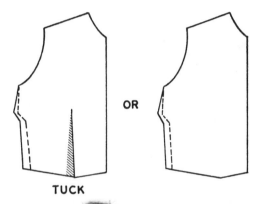

TUCK

Fig. 45.   To make a blouse waist smaller.

B. *To make a blouse waist larger:* Add at the side seam or slash the waist back (or front or both if needed) (Fig. 46).

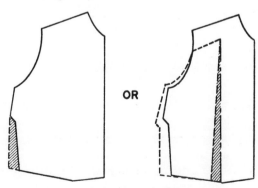

OR

Fig. 46.   To make a blouse waist larger.

VI. Sleeve alterations.

A. *To shorten sleeves:* To shorten the sleeve, take a tuck in the pattern in the desired place. Trim the seam edge even (Fig. 47).

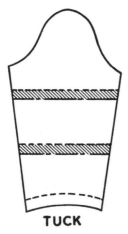

TUCK

Fig. 47.   To shorten sleeves.

B. *To lengthen sleeves:* The sleeve may be lengthened either above or below the elbow or in both places if needed. Usually if length is needed, it is required both above and below the elbow. Slash and spread as desired (Fig. 48).

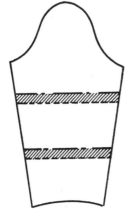

Fig. 48.   To lengthen sleeves.

C. *For a heavy upper arm:* Slash the sleeve pattern beginning about 1 in. from the top and cut toward the wrist. Spread the slash the desired amount. Form darts at the sides of the slash to flatten the pattern. Check the length of the sleeve after alteration. Add length at the cap to compensate for the darts (Fig. 49).

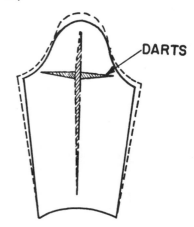

DARTS

Fig. 49.   For a heavy upper arm.

Skirt Alterations

I. Waistline alterations.

A. *To make a skirt waist smaller:* Remove the excess on the seam from the waist to the hip if it is not over

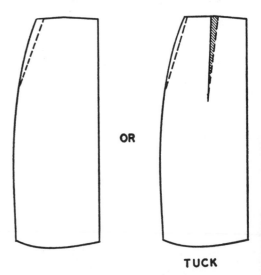

OR

TUCK

Fig. 50.   To make a skirt waist smaller.

¼ in. Take a tuck between the dart and side seam if the excess is over ¼ in. The excess may be removed from the waist to the hip (Fig. 50).

B. *To make a skirt waist larger:* Slash between the dart and the side seam, spreading the slash the desired amount; or, add on the side seam from the top of the skirt to the hip (Fig. 51).

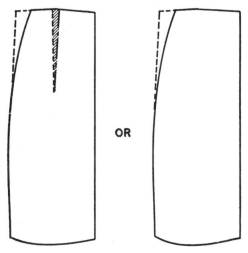

OR

Fig. 51. To make a skirt waist larger.

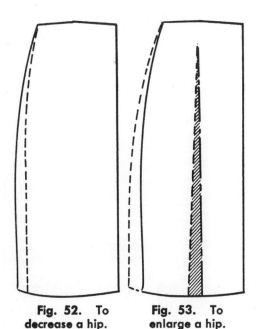

Fig. 52. To decrease a hip.

Fig. 53. To enlarge a hip.

II. Hip alterations.

A. *To decrease a hip:* Trim off the side seams to the desired hip width (Fig. 52).

B. *To enlarge a hip:* Slash on a line parallel to the center front up the middle of the front from the lower edge to ¼ in. from the waistline. To eliminate width at the hem, the side seam may be trimmed slightly beginning at the hipline. Darts may be needed at the waistline (Fig. 53).

III. Length alterations.

A. *To shorten a skirt:* Take a tuck in the pattern, as indicated, to remove the desired length just below the hip. True-up the side line (Fig. 54).

B. *To lengthen a skirt:* Slash the pattern just below the hip as indicated and spread it the desired amount. If the skirt is straight, length may be added at the bottom (Fig. 55).

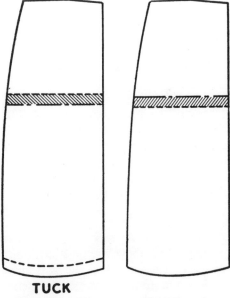

TUCK

Fig. 54. To shorten a skirt.

Fig. 55. To lengthen a skirt.

IV. For a protruding abdomen.

Make an L-shaped slash 7 to 9 in. from the pattern waist at the center front to midway between seams, and slash up to the waist to about ½ in. from the waist. Spread the slash and relocate the center front line. The side seam may have to be relocated as indicated if the width at the skirt hem is more than desired (Fig. 56).

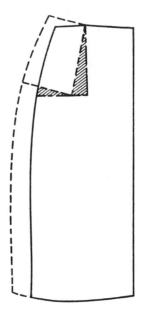

Fig. 57.   For a large thigh.

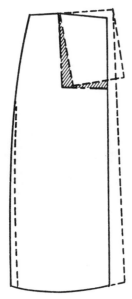

Fig. 56.   For a protruding abdomen.

V. **For a large thigh.**

Slash 7 to 9 in. from the waist from the heavy part of the thigh in to about the center of the pattern and up to about ½ in. from the waistline. Spread the slash and relocate the waist and side seam (Fig. 57).

VI. **For a sway back.**

Take a slight tuck in the blouse about 4 in. above the waistline, tapering it. Take a tuck in the skirt about 3 to 4 in. from the waistline, tapering as indicated (Fig. 58).

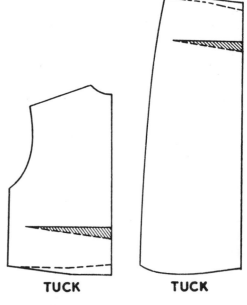

TUCK   TUCK

Fig. 58.   For a sway back.

CHAPTER 8

General Tailoring Techniques

AS THE sailor "swabs the deck" so the tailor "builds a coat." "Laying on fair" refers to making two equal lengths of material coincide. Whereas in dressmaking we usually sew on material, the tailor uses "cloth." Using an ease thread is called *drawing in,* and *fulling on* means easing the longer length of material onto the shorter. The *lapel* refers to the entire front edge of the coat, whereas the *revers* is the part that turns over. When placing the material on the table for cutting, the tailor calls this *laying up the cloth,* which is *on the double.*

To do his work, the tailor adopts a cross-legged position, sitting on his bench, with his work on his knee. He sews with silk thread, since it is more elastic and does not snarl easily, and sews toward himself with short "between" needles.

The tailor's thimble is open at the end, so he pushes the needle through the material on the side of the thimble close to the lower edge. The thread is waxed by passing it through the beeswax, then smoothing it between his fingers. Seams are ended by taking stitches on top of one another, rather than tying a knot.

There are many hand-sewing techniques used in tailoring that should be mastered before tailoring is attempted.

Hand-Sewing Stitches

I. Alteration basting.

A. Basting used when fitting from the right side of the garment and as a guide for machine stitching on the wrong side.

B. Fold the amount to be taken in to the right and pin.

C. Bring the needle up from the wrong side, and catch one or two threads of the folded edge.

D. Place the needle opposite this point and make another stitch parallel to the folded edge about ½ in. long.

E. On the right side there will be small stitches perpendicular to the seam, and on the wrong side, slanting stitches (Fig. 61).

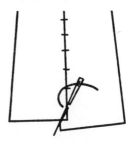

Fig. 61. Basting.

II. Arrowhead stitch.

A. A tack stitch is used to reinforce and decorate the ends.

B. Use matching buttonhole twist.

C. Begin at A, within the tack, and bring the needle out at the base of the triangle (Fig. 62, a).

D. Take a small ⅟₁₆-in. stitch at B, from the right to the left parallel to the base, making a long stitch from A to B (Fig. 62, a).

E. Insert the needle at C and bring it up close to A beside the stitch and

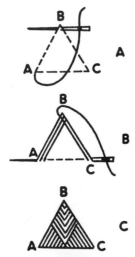

Fig. 62.   An arrowhead stitch.

repeat until the stitches from A to C meet at the center and the stitches across widen out from the ⅟16-in. stitch at the point, ending halfway down the sides (Fig. 62, b).

F. Fasten on the wrong side.

G. The stitches should be even and close to one another so that the fabric does not show through (Fig. 62, c).

III. Backstitch.

A. A stitch used where an especially strong seam is desired, for example, the center back seam of trousers, a sleeve seam, or parts that might be difficult to reach with the machine, or for edge finishing.

B. Take a stitch from right to left. Point the needle toward the left, bringing it up twice the length of the finished stitch.

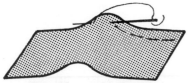

Fig. 63.   A backstitch.

C. For the next stitch, insert the needle close to the last stitch and again bring it up twice the length of the stitch (Fig. 63).

D. A *slanting* backstitch is used to sew on patch pockets from the wrong side. The needle is inserted near the pocket edge and is brought out a stitch length from the edge forming a diagonal stitch. Pull the stitches taut. Repeat this process doing a second row approximately ¼ in. inside of the first row (Fig. 64).

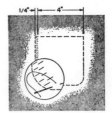

Fig. 64.   A slanting backstitch.

IV. Bar tack.

A. A tack used to reinforce the mouth of pockets.

B. Use buttonhole silk twist.

C. Make three or four bars or satin stitches (Fig. 65, a).

D. Work rotary prick stitches around the entire length, barely stitching the fabric. Sometimes a buttonhole stitch is used around the satin stitches (Fig. 65, b).

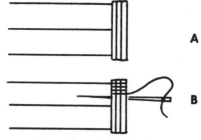

Fig. 65.   A bar tack.

V. Blind and buttonhole stitches.

A. For blind stitch see p. 149.

B. For buttonhole stitch see p. 115.

VI. Catch stitch.

A. A stitch used in hemming or putting darts in a lining (Fig. 66).

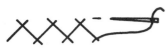

Fig. 66. A catch stitch.

B. Work from left to right. Point the needle toward the left (Fig. 66).

C. A *running* catch stitch is used to attach the lining hem at the coat and sleeve bottom and to attach the coat-facing seam to the interfacing underneath the facing. The running catch stitch is the same stitch which is used for the tailor's hem for hemming skirts and coats, with or without seam binding. It is desirable since it is one of the least conspicuous of all methods of hemming (Fig. 67).

Fig. 67. A running catch stitch.

VII. Drawing-in stitch.

A. A stitch used on the lower half of the armhole to "draw in" or "cup" the underarm seamline.

B. Use strong basting cotton. It may be doubled and twisted.

C. Knot the thread and insert it at A, taking a stitch from right to left at B (Fig. 68). Throw the thread around the point of the needle and pull out the needle, throwing the thread toward the right to complete the stitch (Fig. 68).

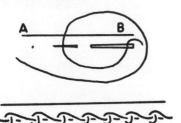

Fig. 68. A drawing-in stitch.

VIII. Even basting.

A. Stitching used for holding material together firmly before stitching.

B. Make equal-size running stitches about ¼ to ½ in. in length (Fig. 69).

Fig. 69. Even basting.

IX. Felling stitch.

A. A stitch used to fasten the tape to the canvas and to attach the under-collar to the coat.

B. Work from right to left, catching a yarn of the canvas and then the tape. The needle is inserted in a slanting position.

C. The stitches will be slanted on both the right and wrong sides (Fig. 70).

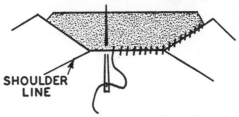

SHOULDER LINE

Fig. 70. Felling stitch. (Note: Stitch enlarged on drawing.)

X. Guide basting.

A. Stitching used to mark the center front or the center back of a garment or any grainline location.

B. Make a running stitch with a long float on the right side (Fig. 71).

Fig. 71. Guide basting.

XI. Hand-pick stitch or uneven backstitch.

A. A stitch used as an edge-finishing stitch for bulky fabrics. The length of the top stitch may be varied from a prick to ⅛ in.

B. Use matching buttonhole twist.

C. With the garment right side toward you, take a tiny backstitch, pushing the needle diagonally through layers of fabric and picking up a tiny stitch on the underside. Bring the needle out on the right side. Repeat the backstitch, keeping the stitches evenly spaced (Fig. 72).

D. This is an excellent stitch for attaching a lining to a garment, particularly for the shoulder, neck, and armscye seam because of its strength.

Fig. 72.   A hand-pick stitch.

XII. Invisible tack.

A. A tack used to reinforce the corners of the welt pocket, i.e., the outside breast pocket.

B. Close the backstitch from the wrong side and do not go through to the right side.

XIII. Overcasting.

A. Used to prevent seams from raveling.

B. Work from the right to the left, keeping the stitches as evenly slanted as possible.

C. Stitch diagonally about ¼ in. apart (Fig. 73).

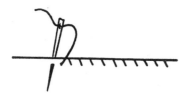

Fig. 73.   Overcast stitch.

XIV. Over-and-Over stitch.

A. A stitch used to reinforce the gorge-

line, to fasten threads, and to fasten the corner of patch pockets from the wrong side.

B. Go over and over on the place to be reinforced.

C. Make another set of stitches across the first, forming a cross-stitch (Fig. 74).

Fig. 74.   An over-and-over stitch.

XV. Pad stitching.

A. Stitching used to fasten the canvas to the facing of the revers, and the collar canvas to the undercollar.

B. Insert the needle horizontally to the left, making stitches ½ to ¾ in. in length.

C. Continue in up and down rows. Do

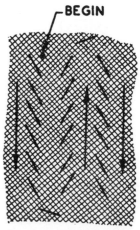

Fig. 75.   Pad stitching.

not turn the fabric as the stitching is reversed.

D. On the inside of the garment, the stitches are vertical rows of diagonal stitches and on the wrong side they are very faint pricks or none at all show (Fig. 75).

XVI. Saddle stitch.

A. A stitch used as an edge finish. The top stitches are longer than those used for a stab stitch or hand-picked stitch.
B. Use matching buttonhole twist.
C. Take stitches one by one as long as desired.

XVII. Stab stitch.

A. A stitch used on areas too thick for a backstitch, and in sewing on buttons and shoulder pads.
B. Prick the needle through the cloth downward all the way, then upward. Keep the needle at right angles to the cloth.
C. From the right side the stitches resemble small dots.

XVIII. Swing tack (French tack).

A. A tack used to hold two edges together loosely, as the coat lining to the coat hem.
B. Sew three or four stitches, with buttonhole twist attaching the lining and garment hem opposite each other, leaving the twist ¾ to 1 in. in length. (Six or eight strands of heavy-duty thread may be substituted.)
C. Buttonhole around these threads for the entire length, keeping the stitches close together (Fig. 76). Sometimes

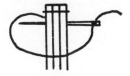

Fig. 76. A swing (French) tack.

a blanket stitch is substituted for the buttonhole stitch.

XIX. Tailor basting (diagonal).

A. Basting used to hold the canvas to the fabric, pockets in position, etc.
B. Insert the needle horizontally to the left with a short stitch.
C. A short vertical stitch appears on the underside and a long slanting (diagonal) stitch on the top (Fig. 77).

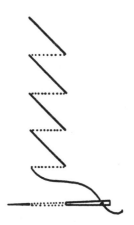

Fig. 77. Tailor basting (diagonal).

XX. Tailor's tacks.

A. Tacks used to transfer temporary markings from the pattern onto the material.

Fig. 78. Tailor's tacks.

B. Using a long double thread of basting cotton, darning cotton, or contrasting colored thread, mark through both pattern and fabric.

C. Take a second stitch in the same place, but allow the thread to form a loop about ½ in. in length.

D. On the printed markings make a stitch 2 in. apart forming a float. Clip the floats and the loops before removing the pattern (Fig. 78).

E. Carefully pull apart the two layers of fabric, and cut the threads between the layers, leaving the cut ends of the thread between the layers of the fabric.

Pressing

Pressing is one of the most important procedures used in tailoring, and it requires time, patience, and practice. It enhances the good features of the garment and can often minimize the defects.

There are many procedures and kinds of equipment used in pressing during the tailoring of a garment. Below are some helpful hints that will make this operation somewhat easier.

I. Definitions.

A. Shrinking.

1. A process used to prepare wool fabric before cutting (see Chapter 6, p. 20) or to change the shape of the fabric as at the top of a sleeve.

2. In the process the length or width of the cloth fibers is decreased to make the length or width of the piece of cloth uniform. It is also used at the top of the sleeve to bring the warp and filling yarns closer together to fit over the shoulder curve.

B. Pressing.

1. Pressing defined.

a. A process used to form creaselines, flatten the edges of a garment, and restore the texture of the fabric and garment.

b. Attempt to maintain the warp and filling threads at right angles in the body of the garment.

2. Kinds of pressing.

a. *Off-pressing:* A process in which the garment is pressed lightly after sponging, the iron being raised from the material to allow the steam to raise the nap. The cloth is shaken lightly.

b. *Underpressing:* Opening and pressing each seam as completed, using the point of the iron. The curved areas are shaped and the edges are flattened.

c. *Top-pressing:* Final pressing on the right side. A press cloth is always used.

d. *Finger-pressing:* A type of underpressing, usually used for seams. The seam is opened with moistened fingers, and pressed when open.

C. *Ironing:* Moving an iron flat along the fabric surface to smooth it. This technique is not used in tailoring.

II. Equipment.

A. Iron. For a description, see Chapter 3, p. 6.

B. Pressing boards. See Chapter 3, pp. 5–7. Pressing boards include beater, ironing board or skirt board, cheese block, cloth press mitt, edge presser, sleeve board, seam roll, tailor's ham, and velvet or needle board.

C. Press cloth and sponge. See Chapter 3, pp. 6–7.

III. Pressing characteristics of wool.

A. Wool is elastic and easily molded or shaped.

B. It will retain its shape when moisture, heat, and pressure are used.

C. If pressure is not applied long

enough, the fabric will not hold its new "set."

D. If pressed too long and too dry, the fibers become "dead," and may begin to decompose or scorch.

IV. Technique.

A. The surface of the fabric which is to be pressed — press on the wrong side, except when top pressing is needed for finishing details.

B. Temperature — use a temperature of 350 to 375 deg., medium low, or wool on the iron indicator.

C. Use of a press cloth.

1. Dry iron.

a. *Optional*: Use a damp wool press cloth under the fabric to provide steam and to keep from flattening the wool and ruining the appearance of the surface.

b. On top, place a dry wool cloth and a cotton cloth. The dry cloth prevents the wool from becoming steam-soaked. Either wet and wring out the cotton cloth or sponge it to make a "steam cloth."

c. *Optional*: Use a dry cloth on top to protect the hand from steam.

2. Steam iron.

a. Use a dry wool pressing cloth on top of the fabric.

b. Place a dry cotton or linen cloth on top of this.

c. *Optional*: A slightly damp wool press cloth may be placed under the fabric and the dry cloth sponged if more steam is needed.

D. Helpful hints.

1. Press as you sew.

2. Press with the grain using a *lower* and *lift* motion.

3. Lift the iron before the wool is

completely dry, because the fabric may lose its elasticity and decompose. Repeat the lowering and lifting motion overlapping the iron prints. The dry cloth and the linen cloth should not be scorched.

4. Avoid pressing directly on the material even on the wrong side.

5. Spank sharp pleats, seam edges, pocket flaps, lapped seams and plackets. Remove bastings and resteam to remove the basting imprint.

6. Seams can be pressed flat with a strip of brown paper under seam allowances to avoid an edge imprint.

7. Curves in a seamline can be shaped with a tailor's ham. Dart ends, collar shaping, and other curves may be pressed over padded rolling pins, towels, or press mitt.

8. Use an edge pressing board for pressing the front seam open.

9. When shrinking or fulling in material, use a taut thread with fine running stitches to draw up the desired amount. Fasten tightly during shaping. Avoid making creases in the material. Another method used by the tailor is to ease the material with the left hand while shaping. Tip the iron to one side as easing is done to avoid stretching. This is used for flared skirt hems, sleeve caps, and underarm seams.

10. For stretching areas, the wide part of the iron is placed over crosswise threads, exerting a semicircular motion, keeping the tip of the iron at a central point. More pressure will cause more stretching.

11. For scorches, mix salts of lemon

with water into a paste and rub this into the scorched area for a few minutes. Expose the material to the sun, wash it with clear water, and allow it to dry. The process may be repeated if needed.

Another method is to dilute hydrogen peroxide with an equal amount of water and add a few drops of household ammonia. Sponge the stain and rinse well with clear water before pressing. It may be necessary to repeat this procedure.

12. Press *pile* fabrics on a velvet board. For seam edges and hems a dry turkish towel topped with a damp cloth may be used. You may substitute two thicknesses of turkish toweling placed on the ironing board, and one thickness over the garment. Place the iron down lightly; then shape the fabric. You may also steam by placing the iron on its heel with the wet cloth over it. Draw the fabric lightly in front of it.

13. For cloth which shines easily, it may be helpful to wring press cloth out of a solution of water and vinegar using approximately one tablespoon of vinegar to one cup of water.

Select General Procedure to Be Used

You are now ready to select the general procedure which you will use to tailor your custom-made garment. If your garment has a notched collar and is a fitted or boxy style suit, you will select Method A, "Procedure for Making a Suit Jacket or Coat With the Lining Sewn in by Hand." Method B, "Procedure for Making a Suit Jacket or Coat With Part of the Lining Sewn in by Machine," is preferred for men's sport jackets or women's boxy, lightly fitted jackets or blazer jackets. You may select Method C, "Procedure for Making a Suit Jacket or Coat With a Shawl Collar," for one in which the collar is cut with the facing and seamed at the center back.

The general procedure sheets are located inside of the back cover of the book for your convenience. Fold out the general procedure you choose to use. Refer to the page references for each step as you proceed with your garment.

CHAPTER **9**

Cutting, Marking, and Staying

Before cutting the wool cloth, many people prefer to make and fit a muslin garment to overcome any fitting problems or intricate designs. However, one must realize that muslin does not drape like wool or have the weight of wool. Below are the steps in laying out and cutting the garment.

I. Lay out the cloth.

A. Examine the cloth carefully and mark all slubs, flaws, discolorations, or damage spots.

B. Be sure the material is completely dry.

C. Lay the fold away from you for easy handling of the material.

D. Shake and run the yardstick through the entire length of the cloth from the selvage to the fold.

E. Pat the two thicknesses together (referred to as "jumping"). "Never fight with the material."

F. Remember that the right side of the wool is on the inside when it comes from the mill.

G. Check to see that the fold of the cloth is on the true grain.

II. Lay the pattern on the cloth.

A. Check the pattern guide sheet for the location of the pattern pieces. Lay all pieces on the material.

B. If the cloth has a *nap*, cut it with the nap running down and place all pattern pieces with the tops facing one end of the cloth. Examples of these fabrics are: cashmere, fleece, wool broadcloth, camel's hair, and panné velvet.

NOTE: *The direction of the most smoothness and least resistance is the direction of the nap or pile. If it feels smooth the nap is going down; if it feels rough, the nap is going up.*

C. Material with a *pile* is usually cut with the pile running up for a richer effect. Examples of these fabrics are: velvet, velveteen, and corduroy.

NOTE: A pile fabric refers to a napped fabric with a surface composed of fiber ends standing up in the air. The exceptions to cutting pile up are corduroy for a garment to be given hard wear and imitation fur fabrics, which are cut down.

D. If the cloth has a *plaid design*, match the plaids both crosswise and lengthwise. Use the same portion of the plaid for the front and back centers.

E. If the plaid is irregular and has an *up and down* or *left and right*, decide which is the "up," and place the pieces of the pattern so that the tops are toward one end of the fabric and also match crosswise and lengthwise.

F. If the two fronts or backs of the pattern are *not identical*, place the pattern pieces on the right side of the unfolded fabric to prevent cutting one section wrong side out.

G. If the cloth is *twill*, the diagonal line will run from the left side toward the right in the front, and from the right to the left in the back.

H. Allow enough room around the pieces for tailor's cutting alterations.

I. Place the *undercollar* pattern on the bias.

41

III. Pin pattern pieces on the cloth.

A. Using sharp pins, pin the grainline and fold of the material, smoothing out the pattern, and pinning edges.

B. Curves and pointed edges require more pins.

C. Pins do not pucker the cloth as much if placed at right angles to the cutting edge.

IV. Cut out the garment, making tailor's cutting alterations.

A. The tailor uses No. 5 cutting shears with bent handles for cutting. He rubs the shears on his hair to prevent sticking.

B. Cut with long even strokes, placing the left hand on the pattern close to the cutting edge and cutting on the right edge of the pattern so that you can always see the edge of the pattern. Do not push while cutting.

C. Novices should cut notches outward but the tailor often folds the edge and cuts out a piece or chalks the markings.

D. The following cutting alterations are suggested for coats and heavier fabrics. These may be *decreased for lighter weight fabrics and designs which accent the "slim look."* It is a great help when fitting to have extra material available at the shoulders, neck, and side seams. European tailors often have 1½- to 2-in. finished seams in their garments. Chalk or pin-mark the alterations before cutting. *Less allowance will be needed if a muslin was fitted.*

  1. Coat.

      a. Add ¾ in. on the *facing* revers tapering from nothing at the top button to the revers point and the back to the gorgeline. Also add ¾ in. on the shoulder if some is added on coat front in this area (Fig. 81, a).

b. For cutting facings on men's sport coats, see Figure 81, b.

c. Add on the facing of a shawl collar as indicated according to the thickness of the material (Fig. 81, c).

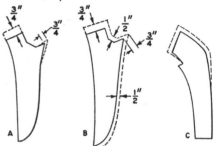

Fig. 81. Coat cutting alterations.

  c. Tailors often add on to *hips* regardless of measure.

  d. The *undercollar* should have a seam at the center back and be cut on the bias, the same size as the pattern. In hard-tailored garments the undercollar is cut of melton rather than wool cloth. Some patterns are designed with the *upper collar* larger so one need not add an extra allowance when cutting.

  e. The upper collar has ½ in. added around the three cut edges on a man's sport coat and blazers (Fig. 82). The outer edge of the collar on the fold is swung out ¼ in. (less on lighter weight material), with the neck edge of the

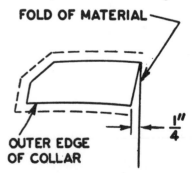

FOLD OF MATERIAL

OUTER EDGE OF COLLAR

Fig. 82. Upper collar alterations for men's sport coats and blazers.

fold on the fold line. *Do not add on the neck edge of shawl collars and dressmaker coats and suits.*

f. For a higher, fuller bust, add 1¼ in. at the shoulder and at the armhole for a larger dart and at the bottom of armhole (Fig. 83).

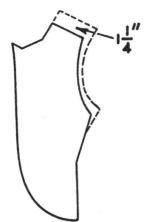

Fig. 83.   For a higher, fuller bust.

g. For a raglan sleeve, add 1 to 1½ in. at the shoulders to allow for shoulder alterations and shoulder pads.

h. Add ¾ to 1¼ in. on the shoulder of the front and back, the amount depending on the

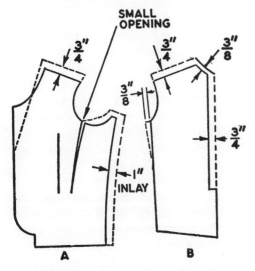

Fig. 84.   For a man's sport coat.

weight of the material and the design of the pattern.

i. Allow 1 to 1½ in. for the underarm seams of coats and suit jackets, and 1 in. for skirts.

j. If the figure is round in back, some allowance may be made at the back of the neck.

k. For cutting a man's sport coat see Figure 84.

l. Some tailors add ¾ to 1 in. at the top of the sleeve tapering to the notches for fitting (Fig. 85).

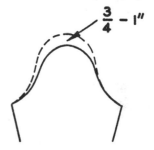

Fig. 85.   Sleeve tapering.

m. Allow 1½ in. for sleeve hems, 2 to 3 in. for coat hems, and 1 to 1½ in. for jacket hems, in addition to the desired finished length. Some patterns allow less.

n. For additional hints on cutting pockets and collars, see Chapter 14, p. 58; Chapter 22, p. 92; and Chapter 23, p. 96.

2. Lining.

a. Allow 1 to 1½ in. pleat at the center back of the *lining*. If the pattern does not call for it, a pleat may be basted in the lining material on the wrong side and turned toward the left. Baste the folded edge of the pleat flat and use the fold line on the right side for center back when cutting.

b. For a man's sport coat (fully lined), allow ¾ in. for the back pleat, 7 to 8 in. down from the neck; taper to nothing to vent.

c. Some tailors add ½ in. at the

shoulder seam, armscye line, and at the back of the neck.

3. Interlining.

Cut the *interlining* the same as the lining, extending just to the top of the hemline at the coat hem and sleeve hem.

4. Canvas and interfacing.

a. *Canvas* (interfacing or reinforcement) is usually cut of hymo for the front and wigan for the sleeve hems, coat hem, and back.

b. Cut the canvas for the *front* interfacing of hymo, 1 in. wider than the facing at the inner edge. There should be a shoulder-to-bust dart; if there is none, provide one by cutting the shoulder seam 1 in. longer at the neck and armscye edge (Fig. 86A).

c. To cut a canvas for Raglan and Dolman sleeves, see Figure 86B. To cut a canvas for a man's sport coat, see Figure 87.

d. The interfacing for the back is usually cut of wigan or firm muslin. It may be on the bias with a seam down the center, or the center back may be on the warp grainline. The length varies from 4 to 10 in. at the center back

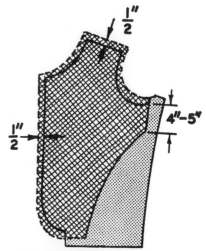

Fig. 87.   Cutting the canvas.

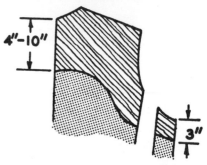

Fig. 88.   Length of wigan.

to 3 in. under armscye (Fig. 88). In a *swing back*, cut the interfacing to fit the wearer, allowing the coat to fall free from the shoulder. A man's coat does not have a back interfacing.

e. Some flared and crisp suit pockets are lined from the waistline to the hem with hymo.

f. Cut the *collar* canvas of hymo, on the bias with a center back seam, the same as the pattern. A high-styled suit pattern may have a bias cut collar with no seam. A man's sport-coat collar is made out of *linen* canvas.

g. In *jacket hems, coat hems,* and *sleeve hems,* cut a true bias interfacing of wigan the width of the hem, plus ½ in., and the

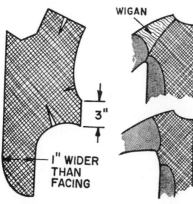

Fig. 86A.
Front
interfacing.

Fig. 86B.
Raglan (top)
and Dolman
(bottom)
sleeves.

length of the circumference plus a seam allowance. Only men's coats sleeve hems are reinforced.

h. For the *skirt belt,* cut a lengthwise strip of canvas half the width of the band plus ½ in.

5. Felt.

Optional: Cut the felt padding for the armhole of cotton felt for hard-tailored garments. Cut a U-shaped piece about 3 in. wide. For some women's garments the felt is cut to fit the front armhole plus a 2- to 3-in. extension at the shoulder.

V. Mark the pattern pieces.

A. Use uneven basting to mark the center front and back of the jacket and the skirt. It is helpful to mark the centers of the skirt, yokes, collars, and the horizontal grain at the base of the sleeve cap.

B. Make the other markings with a tracing wheel and carbon on the wrong side, or use tailor's tacks. Darning cotton or embroidery floss holds well on wool cloth for markings.

C. Mark the following:
1. Darts, tucks, pleats, gathers, clip marks, ease locations, slash marks; 2. Fold lines; 3. Pattern shoulder line, neck edge, revers edge; 4. Waistline; 5. Buttonholes; 6. High point of the sleeve and top of the shoulder; 7. Underarm placement of the sleeve for hard-tailored garments; 8. Pocket placement; 9. Placement for decorative design or stitching; 10. Placement of the collar onto the garment; 11. Original seamlines where cutting alterations have been made; 12. Seamlines on pocket flaps, belt ends, etc.; 13. Any other markings.

D. Remove the pattern pieces from the cloth.

VI. Stay the garment.

A. Stay-stitch the *neckline* and *side*

seams to prevent the cloth from stretching and to preserve the pattern line. Stay-stitch with matching thread, directional with a regulation stitch. Stitch through a single thickness of fabric ⅛ in. outside the seamline (toward the cut edge). Stay-stitch on the *front* from the shoulder to the gorge and the side seams (if they are off grain) as indicated (Fig. 89). Stay-stitch the back neckline from the shoulder to the center.

NOTE: Remember to stitch from the highest to the lowest and the widest to the narrowest.

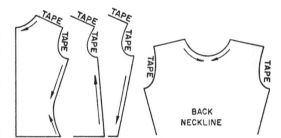

Fig. 89.   Direction of stay-stitching.

B. Baste the stay-tape into the armscye. Place one edge of the tape on the edge where the stitching will be done. The other edge of the tape lies toward the body of the garment, and not on the seam allowance. The lower half of the tape will be removed for shaping and then rebasted. Usually when the interfacing extends into the armscye, the tape is not stitched into the seam but removed. Stitched-in tape should be clipped.

C. Baste the tape into the shoulder seam. Apply tape to the front of the shoulder seam. The darts may be basted in first. The untaped side (back) is then basted to the taped side for fitting. On loose fabrics the tape may be stitched in the final seam. If it is not stitched in, remove it when the final stitching is done.

CHAPTER 10

Constructing Darts and Seams in Tailored Garments

Constructing Darts in a Skirt, Jacket, or Coat

A DART is a fold in the fabric, tapering at either one or both ends. Its purpose is to remove fullness and wrinkles by controlling extra length and width of fabric over body curves between seamlines.

I. Types of darts.
A. One type is wide at one end and tapers to nothing at the other. This is usually a straight dart (Fig. 91, a).

STRAIGHT DART

CURVED DART

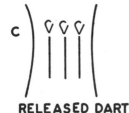

RELEASED DART

Fig. 91. Kinds of darts.

B. Another type is wide in the center and tapers to a point at each end. This dart is often used at the waistline and is a curved dart (Fig. 91, b).
C. Some waistline and shoulder darts are released part of the way (Fig. 91, c).

D. Sometimes darts are made on the right side of the garment for a decorative effect.

II. Location of darts.
A. Front shoulder seam.
   1. Often under the lapel.
   2. Point toward the bust.
B. Back shoulder darts.
   Point toward the shoulder-blade bone.
C. Neckline darts.
   Remove fullness at the neck so that the coat collar will fit snugly.
D. Underarm darts.
   Point toward the tip of the bust.
E. Sleeve darts.
   1. Fall at the seam over the elbow to give room for the elbow to bend.
   2. If there are three darts, the center one falls at the tip of the elbow.
F. Waistline darts.
   1. This type usually tapers at both ends.
   2. The widest part should fall at the natural waistline.
G. Skirt darts.
   1. Taper at the bottom.
   2. The fullness of the dart turns toward the center back or center front.

III. Marking darts.
A. Transfer the dart markings from the pattern to the cloth with the tracing wheel and carbon or use tailor tacks (see Chapter 9, p. 45, "Cutting, Marking, and Staying").

B. Mark the darts on the wrong side of the fabric.

IV. Pinning and basting the marked darts.

A. Work from the narrow end to the wide end. Crease the fold and match the markings exactly. Pin and baste.

B. Do not stretch or twist the fabric because one side may be more on the bias than the other.

C. If one side is more curved, ease it onto the other side.

V. Stitching darts.

A. Stitch from the wide end to the narrow end (Fig. 92).

END

Fig. 92.   Stitching darts.

B. At the end, *stitch from ⅛ to ¼ in. from the edge parallel to the fold, tapering to just one or two yarns from the edge.* This prevents a pucker at the end of the dart.

C. For a curved dart, begin at either end.

VI. Fastening the ends of darts. (Use one of the methods listed below.)

A. Backstitching.
Retrace the stitches from ¼ to ½ in.

B. Back-tacking.
At the end of the stitching line, hold the fabric in front of the presser foot, and using the hand on the balance wheel, place several stitches over each other.

C. Tying a square knot.
1. Pull the threads to the wrong side or to the same side of the dart by pulling on one thread until a loop forms. Insert a pin or needle in the loop and pull the thread.
2. Tie the threads in a square knot.

a. Place the right over the left for the first knot.
b. Place the left over the right for second knot.
3. Cut the ends about ½ in. from the knot.

D. Carry the ends back with the needle.
1. Thread the ends into a needle and carry them between the layers of the cloth for about 2 in.
2. Clip close to the surface of the cloth.

E. Stitching by machine without a knot.
1. Thread the bobbin thread through the needle in reverse.
2. Tie it to the spool thread and wind the knot on the spool with enough thread to stitch the dart.
3. Stitch the dart from the point end with a continuous thread.
4. This method is recommended for decorative darts on the outside of the garment.

VII. Finishing darts on the wrong side.

A. Narrow darts.
1. If a dart is ¼ in. or less in width, do not cut it open.
2. Thin fabrics often are just pressed.
3. The material may be pressed flat to form a box pleat (Fig. 93, a).
4. Some narrow darts may be cut ½ to 1 in. from the narrow end. Press the uncut end in a box pleat. Press open the cut portion (Fig. 93, b).

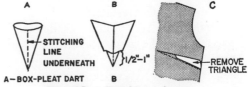

A   B   C
STITCHING LINE UNDERNEATH
½"–1"
A—BOX-PLEAT DART   B
REMOVE TRIANGLE

Fig. 93.   Finishing darts.

B. Wide darts.
1. Trim wide darts to the seam width, press open. Press the uncut portion at the bottom in a box pleat as in Figure 93, b above.

2. On gauzy woolens or white garments where the dart shows through and the bulk needs to be removed, cut along the fold line of the dart to about ½ in. from the point. Cut along the stitching line through the top layer only about ¼ in. from the stitching until it meets the first slash, removing a triangle of a single layer of fabric. This removes the bulk, yet from the right side of the garment it looks like a full dart (Fig. 93, c).

C. Curved darts.

1. If the dart is wide, cut it open, and press.
2. If the dart is narrow, slash from ⅛ to ¼ in. from the stitching line in two or three places in the wide section.

VIII. Pressing darts.

A. Press darts on the wrong side first, on the stitching, then on right side.
B. Turn all front vertical darts toward the center front and back vertical darts toward the center back.
C. Press darts before stitching into a seam.
D. Place a folded strip of brown paper between the dart and the garment to prevent imprints on the right side of the garment.
E. Press over a ham to shape, carefully shrinking the areas at the ends of the dart.

Seams Used for Tailored Garments

Straight, even, "plumb" seams are a necessity for the garment with the "custom look." The types of seams used for suits and coats are explained below.

I. The purpose of seams.
Seams are used to hold two or more pieces of fabric together.

II. Types of seams.

A. *Plain seam.* A seam used mostly for suits and coats.

1. Place two right sides together with the edges even and the notches matched.
2. Pin and baste. When correct, machine-stitch and press open (Fig. 94, a).
3. Sometimes this seam is topstitched

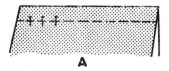

A

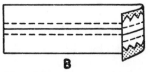

B

Fig. 94. Plain seams.

from the right side for a decorative effect or added strength (Fig. 94, b).

B. *Welt.* Used for "hard tailoring," i.e., for the back seam of the coat, side seams, and the top of the armscye seam.

1. Make a plain seam on the wrong side of the fabric.
2. Turn both edges to the same side. Press.
3. Trim the seam edge next to the garment.
4. Baste the desired width from the seamline. Stitch on the right side along the basting (A, Fig. 95).
5. Press.
6. Another row of stitching may be placed along the seam line at B, Figure 95.

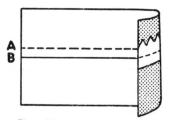

Fig. 95. A welt seam.

C. *Lapped seam.* A seam used on yokes.
1. Turn under one edge of the fabric on the seamline and press.
2. Lap the turned edge onto the other edge so that the raw edges meet and the marked seamline meet.
3. Stitch on the right side near the folded edge. The stitching may be on the fold, ⅛ to ¼ in. from edge (Fig. 96).

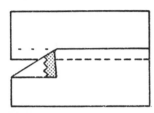

Fig. 96.   A lapped seam.

D. *Flat-fell seam.* A seam used for boys' suits and sport coats.
1. Place two wrong sides together, baste, and stitch the desired seam width.
2. Turn both edges in the same direction. Press.
3. Trim underneath the seam to about one half of the desired finished seam.
4. Turn under the upper seam allowance. Keep a uniform distance from the seamline. Baste, press, and stitch down flat to the garment along the folded edge. Press (Fig. 97).

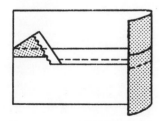

Fig. 97.   A flat-fell seam.

E. *Slot seam.* A seam used on the back of coats, and for skirts.

1. Crease along both cut edges and turn under. Baste over the underlay, either having folded the edges together or slightly apart as desired. Stitch as far as desired from the folded edge (Fig. 98A).

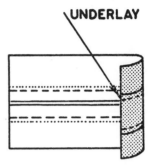

Fig. 98A.   A slot seam.

2. A simulated slot seam can be made by pressing a plain seam open. Each side of the seam may be topstitched (Fig. 98B).

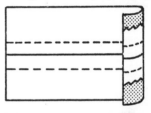

Fig. 98B.   A simulated slot seam.

F. *Corded seam.* A seam used on the edges of collars and pockets.
1. Cut a strip of bias wide enough to go around the cord plus two seam allowances. The cord may be purchased at a notion counter or heavy string which is shrunk may be used.
2. Place the bias around the cord right side out and machine-baste with the cording foot close to the

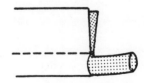

Fig. 99A.   Making a corded seam.

cord, using matching thread (Fig. 99A).

3. Place the covered cord on the right side of the fabric so the machine line matches the marked seamline. The seam allowance of the cord is on top of the garment seam allowance (Fig. 99B).

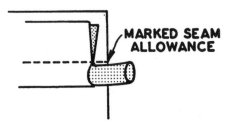

MARKED SEAM ALLOWANCE

Fig. 99B.   Making a cord seam.

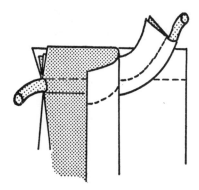

Fig. 99C.   Completing the cord seam.

4. Make the seam by placing two right sides of the garment together. Baste and stitch along the seamline (Fig. 99C).

G. *Taped seam.* A seam used on garments of loose-weave fabric that stretches or for bias seams. Linen tape, selvedge, or twill tape may be used. Dalman, raglan, and kimono sleeves and center back bias seams may be reinforced also.

1. Baste the tape to the already basted seam. Baste so that when machine-stitched, the stitching will catch the tape (Fig. 100).

2. Stitch the basted tape and seam.

Fig. 100.   A taped seam.

III. Hints in handling seams:

A. *Eased seam:*
The back shoulder seam, which is slightly longer than the front seam, is eased onto the front seam. Pin, baste, and stitch with the eased seam (back) uppermost.

B. *Napped cloth to plain cloth:*
Pin and baste the plain fabric to the napped material (napped surface up). Stitch with the plain fabric uppermost.

C. *Straight to bias material:*
Pin, baste, and stitch the bias cloth on top of the straight.

D. *Crossed seams:*
When two seams cross, trim one seam diagonally from the seam edge toward the stitching line to remove bulk (Fig. 101, a and b). For heavy fabrics, clip seam ⅛ to ¼ in. from stitching line. Trim seam out in a V (Fig. 101, c).

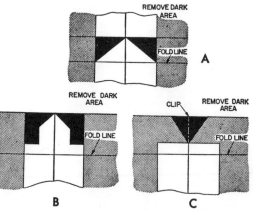

Fig. 101.   Removing bulk from crossed seams.

CHAPTER 11

Constructing Interfacing and Canvas

IN HARD tailoring the reinforcement used in the forepart of the coat is referred to as the "canvas" while in softly tailored garments it is more often known as an "interfacing." At any rate, the canvas is the foundation of the coat, and should be shaped to fit the wearer. When properly constructed and attached, it assists in keeping the garment in shape, giving it the "custom-tailored" look.

For a man's sport coat a ready-made canvas, including the collar canvas, can be purchased. It may have to be recut to fit the coat. Also, some tailors will cut out a simple canvas for the tailoring student to construct or one can be made.

Constructing Reinforcement for Women's Suits and Coats

I. Slash and pin the shoulder darts.

A. Slash from the middle of the shoulder to the point of the bust (Fig. 103A). The reinforcement may be held up to the figure or checked with fitted pattern for the location of the bust.

B. Lap the cut edges until there is sufficient ease over the bust area. Pin.

II. Slash and pin the armscye darts.

A. Slash a dart about 1¼ to 1⅝ in. long and ⅜ in. wide from the lower front armscye toward the tip of the bust. The amount taken out varies with the individual figure (Fig. 103A).

B. Lap and pin the edges.

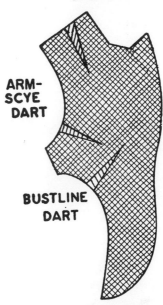

SHOULDER DART

ARM-
SCYE
DART

BUSTLINE
DART

Fig. 103A.   Darts.

C. This is the area where the coat is held in, so this armscye dart corrects the fit of the canvas in this area.

III. Slash and pin the bustline darts.

A. The bustline dart is often used on women's fitted suits.

B. It is located from the tip of the bust vertical to the lower inner edge of the reinforcement (Fig. 103A).

C. Lap and pin.
NOTE: Shape the interfacing for a full-length coat to prevent the bottom of the coat from swinging out. Slash the interfacing at the waistline horizontally for 2 in. then vertically

to just below the tip of the bust. Slash upward to (Fig. 103B) within 1½ to 2 in. from the tip of the bust. Remove triangle A which is 1 in. at base. Using this triangle as a pattern, place it along the inner edge of the canvas and remove the other triangle B, the same size (Fig. 103B). Bring the raw edges together and stitch as in IV, B below.

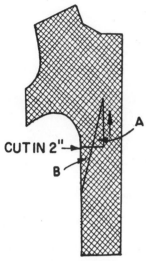

Fig. 103B.   Interfacing for full-length coat.

IV. Stitch the darts.

A. If the reinforcement is of lightweight material, you may lap the cut edges, lapping the front edge of the dart over the back edge and zigzag stitch over the edge (Fig. 104A).

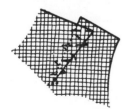

Fig. 104A.   Stitching the dart. (Dart slashed in center.)

B. When hymo is used most tailors cut on the marked dart lines, removing the dart. A piece of bias wigan,

silesia, or muslin (or lengthwise grain may be used) about ¾ to 1 in. wide and about an inch longer than the dart is placed behind the dart. Bring the cut dart edges together so they meet on top of the strip and zigzag stitch in position. Stitch along the edges first if desired. Sometimes, after straight stitching, the dart is catchstitched by hand instead of zigzagging by machine (Fig. 104B).

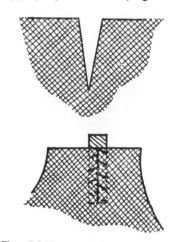

Fig. 104B.   Another method of stitching a dart. (Dart removed.)

NOTE: The canvas at this point is ready to be applied to the coat for the first fitting.

V. Attach the cotton felt (optional).

NOTE: Attach after the first fitting and shaping of the canvas (see Chapter 16, p. 77).

A. The cotton felt is used on hard-tailored garments and coats to protect the body from the hymo and help the garment retain its shape.

B. Place the felt, which is about 1½ to 2 in. wide, on top of the hymo. Bring it to the seam at the underarm and allow it to extend loosely at the shoulders so that later it may extend onto the back reinforcement (Fig. 105A).

C. Dart the felt with a scye dart to correct the fit at this point (Fig. 105A).

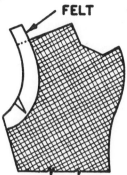

Fig. 105A. Adding felt.

D. On a man's coat, the felt is cut to fit the entire armscye without an underarm seam (Fig. 105B).

E. Pad-stitch the felt into position.

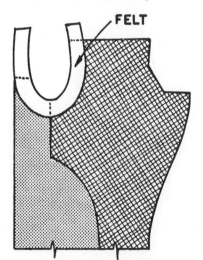

Fig. 105B. Adding felt to a man's coat.

Constructing Reinforcement for Men's Suit Coats

(Simple design for the beginner)

I. Cut the canvas according to the pattern and slash the shoulders and armscye.

Cut the canvas of hymo or armo and slash about 3 in. in length where there normally would be a shoulder dart and twice in the armscye area (Fig. 106).

Fig. 106. Darts for man's coat.

II. Cut a second piece of armo for the hollow of the shoulder.

A. Cut this piece about ½ in. within the creaseline, about 12 to 14 in. long (Fig. 107).

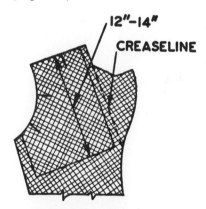

Fig. 107. Piece for the hollow of the shoulder.

B. Slash at the middle and lower part of the scye line and shoulder.

C. These slashes are not lapped but left loose.

III. Cut another piece of lightweight woolen material.

A. Cut this piece also ½ in. within the creaseline, 11 to 12 in. long (Fig. 108).

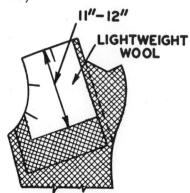

Fig. 108. Cutting the lightweight wool.

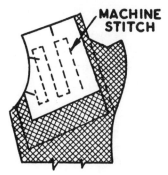

Fig. 109. Fastening the three pieces together.

B. Make a slash at the shoulder and two slashes at the armscye.

IV. **Fasten the three layers together.**
Use machine stitching (Fig. 109).

V. **Attach the bridle.**

A. Use a straight piece of linen, or strong cotton about ⅜ to 1 in. wide, and machine-sew on both sides of tape along the crease.

B. Place this on the creaseline to cover the raw edges of the smaller piece of hymo and wool material.

VI. **Attach the cotton felt.**

A. The cotton felt may be attached to the forepart after the canvas is shaped (Fig. 105B).

B. Use either a U-shaped felt piece or one shaped to fit the front armhole and extend above the shoulder about 2 in.

Directions for another type of tailor's canvas for a man's suit coat may be found in Poulin, *Tailoring Suits the Professional Way,* pp. 56–60.*

---

* Clarence Poulin, *Tailoring Suits the Professional Way* (Peoria: Chas. A. Bennett Co., Inc., 1952), pp. 56–60.

CHAPTER 12

Preparing for the First Fitting

IF A muslin garment has been fitted and altered, this first fitting may be less difficult. The wool, however, does drape and mold differently from muslin, which makes this first fitting important in order to produce the garment with the "custom look."

Having cut, marked, and stayed the garment, it is now basted for try-on.

Basting-Up the Garment

I. Baste in the darts (see Chapter 10, p. 47).
A. Baste in the darts, carefully matching the markings.
B. Baste from the widest to the narrowest part of the dart.

II. Baste the coat seams together (see Chapter 10, p. 48, and Chapter 20, p. 87).
A. Baste in all seams.
B. Use *directional* basting, sewing from the widest to the narrowest or the highest to the lowest of each seam.
C. Do not apply *front facings*.
D. If there is a center-back seam, leave it open at the neckline a seam's width to prevent pulling during fitting.

III. Baste the canvas in the coat forepart.

This will be removed after fitting in order to put in the pockets.

IV. Baste on the undercollar.
Lap the raw edges at the seamline.

V. Baste in the sleeves.
A. Baste up the sleeve seams.
B. Baste in the sleeves, easing in the fullness at the cap.

VI. Pin the shoulder pads in position.
The outer edge of the shoulder pad usually extends into the armhole approximately a seam's width beyond the seam line.

VII. Baste up the hem of the coat.

VIII. If a suit is being made, baste the skirt together.
A. Cut, mark, and stay-stitch.
B. Baste up the skirt, putting in the pleats, darts, and side seams.
C. Baste the interfacing in the band and apply the band to the skirt, leaving the ends open and free.

IX. Baste under the seam allowance on the coat front (optional).
This aids the beginner in deciding whether the lapels are the correct width and slope, and in obtaining an idea of the over-all proportions and fit of the garment.

CHAPTER 13

Fitting

THE "custom look" in a suit or coat refers to the appearance of a garment which has been fitted to you, the wearer or home tailoress. Fitting is the technique involved in altering the unfinished garment to fit the wearer properly. For the proper fit of a coat or skirt, see Chapter 41, p. 153. Fitting is probably one of the most difficult problems for the beginner, but once one learns to know his individual fitting problems, it is simply a matter of "cutting to fit." Since the success in making a tailored garment depends on skill in fitting, it is important that you carefully check each item listed below.

Always fit a suit jacket with the skirt on. If a sweater is to be worn under the suit jacket, be sure to wear one for fitting. Also wear the type of foundation for fitting you intend to wear with the finished suit. In fitting a coat, also wear the garment under it that will be worn after it is completed. Pin the closing at the front, lap the center front markings, adjust the garment carefully, and, then, check for fit.

Checking Garment for Fit

I. Check the grain of the material throughout the garment.
A. Across the chest and bust, crosswise yarns should be parallel to the floor.
B. Center front and center back warp-lines should be perpendicular to the floor.

C. Across the back shoulder, the crosswise yarns should be parallel to the floor.

II. **Check the position and direction of the darts.**
A. The front shoulder seam darts should point toward the bust.
B. The back shoulder-blade dart should point toward the shoulder-blade bone.
C. If there are neckline darts, they should remove fullness so that the garment lies smooth at the neckline.
D. The underarm dart should point toward the tip of bust and end about ½ to ¾ in. from the bust point.
E. The sleeve darts fall at the seam over the elbow. If there are three darts, the center one falls at the tip of the elbow.
F. The widest part of the waistline dart should fall at the natural waistline or slightly lower.

III. **Check the direction of the seams.**
The side seams of a jacket and skirt or coat should hang "plumb," and not swing to the back or front.

IV. **Check the neck and the shoulder lines.**
A. The shoulderline should be smooth and follow the fashion and design as to width.
B. The shoulderline should curve slightly (about ¼ in.) into the neck edge so that it will lie smooth.

V. Check the fit of the collar.

The collar should fit closely at the back and sides. The "fall" of the collar should cover the seam at the neck.

VI. Check the breakline of the collar and the roll of the lapel. Mark.

A. Roll the lapel as desired to the top button.

B. The breakline should hug the neck at the back and follow to the lapel roll.

VII. Check the lap of the front edges.

The front edge should hang straight down and should not swing toward the sides.

VIII. Check the sleeves as to grain, width, length, and pitch.

A. The crosswise yarns should be parallel to the floor and lengthwise yarns should be perpendicular to the floor.

B. Check the length of the sleeve. (This may be rechecked at a later fitting).

C. On a hard-tailored garment the sleeves should be pitched so that the sleeve-edge front falls in the center of the mouth of the side pocket.

IX. Check the length of the garment (jacket and skirt or coat).

A. Check the garment for length.

B. Unless fashion dictates otherwise, suit-jacket hems are usually hung evenly from the floor or taper slightly longer in the back.

X. Check buttonhole and pocket locations.

A. Check to see that the location of the buttonholes is desirable. Be sure the top one is not too high or too low. Generally, fitted jackets have a button at the waistline.

B. Check pocket locations as to ease of use, and placement in relation to the figure.

XI. Check any other decorative details.

XII. Mark necessary alterations.

After the alterations are made, the garment is tried on once again and re-checked for fit. Alterations are marked carefully before the garment is taken apart for stitching (see the procedure sheet, Methods A and B — steps 12 and 13).

The number of fittings varies according to the figure and its irregularities, and the skill of the student in tailoring. Often another fitting is made when the collar is attached, another to check the sleeve, and again when shoulder pads are placed in position permanently.

For additional help in fitting coats and suits, see bibliography for suggestions. *Fitting Coats and Suits* by Margaret Smith is recommended for this purpose.

CHAPTER 14

Constructing Pockets

THE flap, welt (Fig. 110A), bound (or slot) (Fig. 110B), and patch (Fig. 110C) pockets are the types most commonly

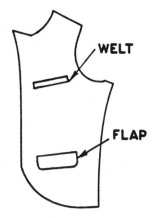

Fig. 110A. Welt and flap pockets.

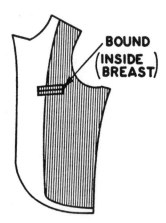

Fig. 110B. A bound or slot pocket.

used in tailored garments. Directions for making other types, such as pockets cut in one with the garment, bellows, and pockets which are set-in darts can be

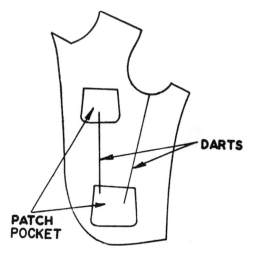

Fig. 110C. Patch pocket.

found in pattern instructions or in dressmaking books.

Since many different methods are used by professional tailors to make pockets, one technique has been chosen for explanation here. Before beginning to construct pockets, familiarize yourself with the following terms: *pocket facing, pouch* or *pocket linings, mouthline, welt,* and *upper* and *under pocket linings* (see p. 4).

Flap Pocket

The location of the pocket was determined during the first fitting. In most cases it is somewhat slanted. The beginner in tailoring usually uses the designed flap that comes in the pattern. The shape of the flap is determined by the design of the coat lapel, collar, and bottom of the front as well as the prevailing style trends.

I. Mark the mouthline.

A. Mark the line with colored thread 1 in. longer than the desired opening. A ruler and thin chalk may be used as a guide in making a straight line.

B. Guide-baste at each end of the mouthline at right angles to it (Fig. 111).

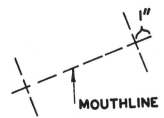

Fig. 111. Guide baste at each end of the mouthline.

II. Cut the flap piece.

NOTE: Omit if the flap was cut from the pattern when the garment was cut out.

A. Cut the flap piece of wool cloth, matching the grainline of the flap to the grainline of the garment.

B. Match the plaids or stripes of the garment, unless a decorative effect is desired.

C. Allow ¼-in. seams at the ends and bottom of the flap and a ½-in. seam at the top (Fig. 112). (If a pattern is used, follow the seamline markings.)

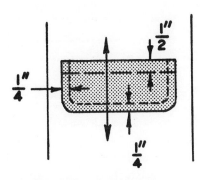

Fig. 112. Pocket seams.

III. Cut the flap lining.

NOTE: Omit if it was cut with the body lining.

A. Cut the lining material exactly like the flap piece.

B. Some tailors cut the flap lining on the bias.

C. Occasionally, this may be of wool.

IV. Cut the flap interfacing.

NOTE: This is used for crisper tailored effects.

Cut the interfacing like the flap minus the seam allowance.

V. Cut the welt.

A. Cut the welt of wool cloth 1½ in. wide and 1 in. longer than the mouthline.

B. The ends will be on the warpwise grain and the lengthwise grain will be parallel to its length.

VI. Cut the pocket pouch.

A. Use silesia, wigan, muslin, flannel, or lining for the pouch.

B. For a straight pocket, cut a single pouch 2 in. wider than the finished pocket and as deep as desired. It should be shorter than the jacket hem if it is a hip pocket.

C. For a slanting pocket, cut two pieces of material 2 in. wider than the mouthline, following the grain of the pocket flap (Fig. 113).

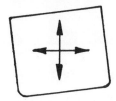

Fig. 113. A slanting pocket pouch.

VII. Cut the pocket facing.

A. Cut of wool (1½ to 2 in. wide) like the welt for a straight pocket.

B. Follow the grainline of the pouch for a slanting pocket (Fig. 114).

C. Sometimes lining is used.

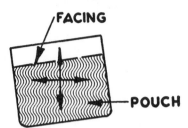

Fig. 114.   Facing for a slanting pocket.

VIII. Cut the pocket stay.

A. Use wigan, silesia, or muslin.

B. Cut the stay 1½ in. wide and 2 in. longer than the mouthline.

IX. Construct the flap.

A. Without interfacing.

1. Be sure that the finished seamlines are marked.

2. Place the wool flap and the flap facing (lining) with the right sides together.

3. Tailor-baste lengthwise through the center (Fig. 115).

4. Pull the wool back ⅟₁₆ in. from the ends and bottom using fine tailor basting (Fig. 115).

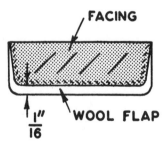

Fig. 115.   Flap for the pocket.

5. Place the material *wool side down* on the machine and stitch ¼ in. (or on marked seamline) from the facing edge on the sides and bottom.

6. If the flap is rectangular, **make one stitch across the corner** to produce a square corner and avoid a knobby appearance (Fig. 116A).

Fig. 116A.   Stitching for a square corner.

7. Trim across angles or notch out curved edges (Fig. 116B).

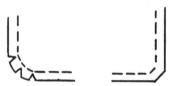

Fig. 116B.   For curved corners.

8. Press the seam open on an edge presser.

9. Turn to the right side, baste around the seam edge, and steam. Remove the bastings and resteam.

10. Edge-stitch if desired.

11. Baste ½ in. from the cut edge of the flap. Ease the lining down to make it ⅟₁₆ in. shorter so that the flap will lie close to the coat (Fig. 117).

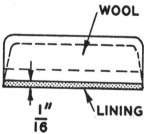

Fig. 117.   Basting the flap.

12. Trim the seam allowance ³⁄₁₆ to ¼ in.

B. With interfacing.

1. Stay-stitch the sides and bottom of the flap with machine stitching

¼₆ in. outside the finished seam line, easing the fabric by stitching (Fig. 118). Do not stay the facing.

INTERFACING

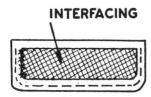

Fig. 118. Stitching the interfacing

2. Catch-stitch the raw edge of the interfacing to the stay stitching on the flap.
3. Proceed from here with the directions above for the construction of a flap without interfacing.

X. Attach the stay.

Baste the stay to the wrong side of the wool, centering it on the mouthline (Fig. 119).

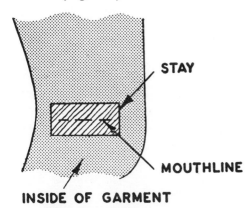

INSIDE OF GARMENT

Fig. 119. Basting the stay.

XI. Attach the welt.
A. Place the welt on the lower edge of the pocket mouthline, centering it, with the two right sides together.
B. For lighter weight fabrics, make the seam about ⅛ in. wide and on heavier fabrics ³⁄₁₆ to ¼ in. wide. A stitching of welt and flap ⅛ in. from the mouthline results in a ¼-in. welt,

whereas stitching the seams ³⁄₁₆ in. from the mouthline results in a ⅜- to ½-in. welt (Fig. 120).
C. Stop the seam ⅛ to ¹⁄₁₆ in. from the vertical guide basting for slanting pockets. Straight pockets may be stitched to the vertical markings (Fig. 120).

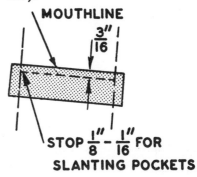

Fig. 120. Attaching the welt.

D. Baste, then stitch, backstitching at each end.

XII. Attach the flap.
A. Place the cut edge of the flap on the mouthline and baste.
B. Stitch on the basting lines. Backstitch at the ends. Be sure to end on vertical guide basting (Fig. 121).

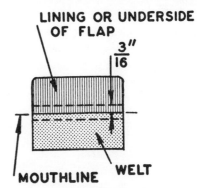

Fig. 121. Attaching the flap.

XIII. Cut the mouthline.
A. Cut only the wool and the stay.
B. Cut on the mouthline to ⅜ to ½ in. from the end (Fig. 122).

C. At the end, cut diagonally to the end of the stitching of the flap and welt to form triangles (Fig. 122).

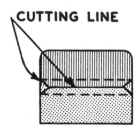

CUTTING LINE

Fig. 122.   Cutting the mouthline.

D. The triangle will not be even on a slanting pocket.

XIV. Press the welt and flap seams.

A. Turn the welt up toward the mouth-line.
B. Press the welt seam open from the wrong side.
C. Press the flap-seam edges upward. Baste.

XV. Stitch in the welt seam.

A. Turn the welt upward toward the mouthline.
B. On the inside turn downward so that the folded edge encloses the edge of welt seam which was pressed open.
C. The welt formed will be ⅜ to ¼ in. wide or less depending on the stitching (see step XI). It may almost fill the space between the stitching but should not crowd the flap.
D. Stitch exactly in the welt and coat seam (Fig. 123).

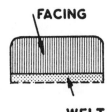

FACING

WELT

Fig. 123.   Stitching the welt seam.

XVI. Attach the facing and top-stitch the flap in position.

A. Turn the flap to downward position. Baste the facing to the seam edges which were pressed upward.
B. Top-baste the flap, easing the coat edge over the seam a scant ⅟₁₆ in. to conceal the flap stitching.
C. Top-stitch ⅟₁₆ in. from the edge (Fig. 124).
D. Remove the bastings.

Fig. 124.   Top-stitching.

XVII. Attach the upper pocket pouch piece to the welt.

A. Use a plain seam joining the welt to the pouch.
B. Press the seam down.

XVIII. Attach the under pocket pouch piece to the facing.

A. Use a plain seam joining the facing to the underpocket pouch.
B. Press the seam upward. Top-stitch along the edge.

XIX. Stitch the under and upper pocket linings to form the pouch.

A. Baste and stitch along the sides catching triangles.
B. The pouch is often made wider at bottom so the flap will lie flatter when inserted in the pocket.

XX. Remove all bastings.

XXI. Finish the ends of the mouthline.

A. You may either backstitch across the ends of mouthline from right side; or:
B. Bar-tack the ends of mouthline.

XXII. Press.

Hard-press first. Lift the flap to off-press, removing flap marks if there are any.

XXIII. Attach the stay.

For a man's sport coat or any garment in which the pockets are strained, a stay may be attached from the end of the pocket nearest the side seam to the armscye. This is done after the canvas is attached to the forepart. Other stays may be placed along the back of the mouthline to the side seam or armscye seam. The stay is catch-stitched at the corners of the mouthline and sewed into the seam (Fig. 125).

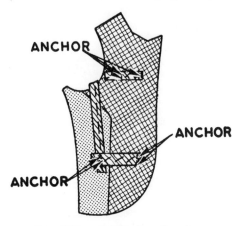

Fig. 125. Anchoring the stays.

NOTE: Some tailors prefer to attach the upper pocket pouch to the welt before it is stitched on to the coat. Likewise, the underpocket pouch is stitched to the facing before it is attached to the coat.

Welt Pocket

I. Mark the position of the pocket.

A. Check to see that the welt slants

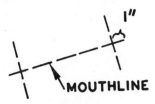

Fig. 126. Mark the mouthline.

downward toward the front of the garment if it is a breast pocket.

B. Mark the desired location with contrasting basting thread, extending 1 in. beyond each end of the mouthline (Fig. 126).

C. Mark each end of the mouthline with vertical basting (Fig. 126).

II. Cut the wool welt.

NOTE: Omit if the pattern piece for welt is used.

A. For a full-length coat, the finished welt is about 7 by 1½ in., and a suit pocket about 5 in. long. This may vary according to prevailing styles.

B. A breast welt pocket finished is about ⅞ in. deep and 3¾ to 4 in. or 1⅛ in. deep by 4½ in. long for men's coats. The armscye end of a breast pocket is on the straight warpline and the other end is curved (Fig. 127).

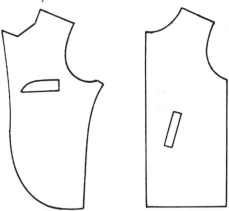

Fig. 127. Welt pockets: left, breast pocket; right, lady's coat pocket.

C. When cutting the welt, allow ¼ to ½ in. for seams.

D. Cut the welt:

1. Mark the finished position of the welt rectangle with heavy blackboard chalk on the coat.

2. Lay the pieces from which the welt is to be cut, right finished side up, matching the grain and design of the fabric.

3. Pat with your hand to transfer the chalk design on the wool from which the welt is to be cut.
4. Fold double from the top chalk-line and cut, allowing ¼- to ½-in. seams on each end and the bottom.
5. If the welt is slanted, the piece will be arrow-shaped (Fig. 128, a); if it is on the straight, it will have straight ends (Fig. 128, b).

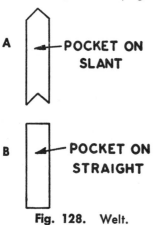

A ←— POCKET ON SLANT

B ←— POCKET ON STRAIGHT

Fig. 128.   Welt.

III. Cut the stay.

A. Use wigan, muslin, or silesia.
B. Cut the stay 1½ in. wide and 2 in. longer than the mouthline.

IV. Cut the pocket pouch.

A. Cut two pieces for the pouch of silesia, lining, or muslin.
B. Cut as deep as desired (about 5 in.) and 1 to 2 in. wider than the length of the mouthline.
C. If the pocket is slanted, cut the pouch on the same slant as the

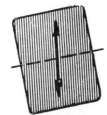

Fig. 129.   Pouch for a slanted pocket.

mouthline, so the grain will lie the same as the coat (Fig. 129).

V. Cut the pocket facing.

A. Cut the pocket facing of wool material.
B. Make the facing 1 to 2 in. wide and 1 in. longer than the pocket mouth-line. The grain should be the same as that of the garment.
C. On a welt pocket for a coat, the wool pocket facing may use the selvage to eliminate a bulky seam (Fig. 130).

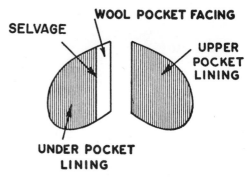

WOOL POCKET FACING
SELVAGE
UPPER POCKET LINING
UNDER POCKET LINING

Fig. 130.   Welt pocket for a coat.

VI. Place the pocket stay in position.

A. Place the pocket stay against the wrong side of the garment, centered on the mouthline.
B. Baste it into position.

VII. Prepare the welt.

A. *Optional:* Stitch one or two lines of stitching ⅛ to ¼ in. from the fold line on the side of the welt next to

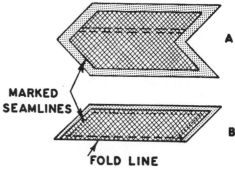

A

MARKED SEAMLINES

B

FOLD LINE

Fig. 131A and B.   Preparing the welt.

the garment. This prevents stretching (Fig. 131A).

B. *Optional:* Interface with hymo or wigan for firmness.

1. The interfacing may be stitched in with the seams and trimmed back. This is a double wool welt (Fig. 131B); or

2. The interfacing may be cut without seams except at the bottom and the wool seam allowance folded over it and catch-stitched (Fig. 131C). The upper pocket

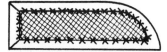

Fig. 131C. Catch-stitched interfacing.

pouch top is shaped like the welt and slip-stitched across the top and around the corner of the welt. The welt is then faced with lining (Fig. 131D).

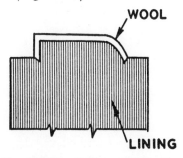

Fig. 131D. Lining on the welt.

3. A double wool welt may be interfaced and constructed by hand also (Fig. 131E).

C. *Stitch the right sides together.* Stitch the ends of the welt on the marked lines, or stitch around the welt on three sides. Trim the seam allowances across the upper corners. Turn the right side out and press. Be sure to roll the seams toward the underside.

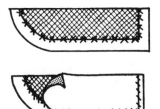

Fig. 131E. A double wool welt.

D. Measure again and run a basting along the stitching line at the bottom of the welt. *Hold the underside of the welt tighter* (Fig. 131F).

E. Top-stitch on the welt if desired.

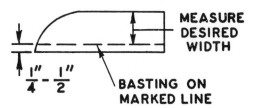

Fig. 131F. Basting the welt.

VIII. Prepare the under-pocket linings.

A. Place the wool pocket facing on the underlining with right sides up.

B. Zigzag stitch the lower edge of the wool or turn under the edge, top-stitch, and press. If selvage, just top-stitch.

IX. Attach the welt.

A. Place the welt on the coat, upside down, right sides together.

B. If the marked seamline at the bottom of the welt is ½ in., the marked

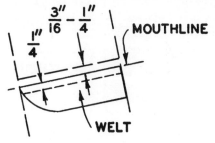

Fig. 132. Attaching the welt.

welt seamline is ¼ in. below the mouthline (see XI, A, B, p. 61) (Fig. 132).

X. Place the upper lining in position.

A. Place the lining on top of the welt so that the stitching line will coincide exactly with the welt stitching line (Fig. 133).

B. Baste into position.

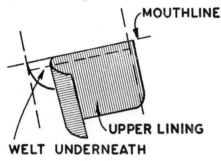

MOUTHLINE

UPPER LINING

WELT UNDERNEATH

Fig. 133.   Adding the upper lining.

XI. Attach the welt and upper lining.

A. Stitch on the marked seamline about ¼ in. down from the mouthline.

B. Stop exactly on the ends of the welt, including it, but not beyond it.

C. Fasten the ends securely.

XII. Place the under pocket lining in position.

A. Wool facing is placed next to the coat on the upper edge of the mouthline (Fig. 134).

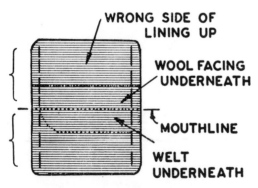

WRONG SIDE OF LINING UP

WOOL FACING UNDERNEATH

MOUTHLINE

WELT UNDERNEATH

Fig. 134.   Adding the under lining — A, upper pocket lining; B, under pocket lining.

B. Raw edges meet the raw edge of the welt (Fig. 134).

C. Baste a ⅛-, ³⁄₁₆-, or ¼-in. seam, depending on the bulkiness of the wool (Fig. 134).

D. Turn the welt into position to **mark** the end of the stitching line. The *ends of underlining stitching must fall just within the ends of the welt* (about ⅛ in. shorter).

XIII. Stitch the underpocket lining.

A. Stitch on the basted seamline.

B. Fasten the ends by retracing or tying the threads securely.

XIV. Cut the pocket mouthline.

A. Cut only the coat fabric and stay.

B. Cut along the center of the mouthline to within ⅜ in. from end (Fig. 135).

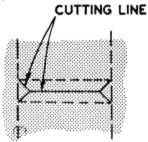

CUTTING LINE

Fig. 135.   Cutting the pocket mouthline.

C. Cut diagonally exactly to the ends of the stitching line.

D. The triangles formed will have one long and one short side if the pocket is slanted.

XV. Complete the pocket pouch.

A. Pull the pocket linings through to the wrong side of the coat, allowing the welt to fall into position. Baste into position, molding to the curve of the figure.

B. Press open the top seam on the wrong side.

C. Allow the triangles to extend into the pocket side under the welt.

D. Clip the seams at the end so that the *welt* seams turn down, and the *underlining* seams turn up.

E. Fasten the triangles by stitching from the wrong side at each end of the mouthline from the bottom of the pocket up, to keep the opening from spreading (Fig. 136).

F. Stitch around the pocket linings to form the pouch.

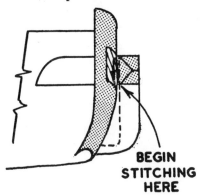

BEGIN STITCHING HERE

Fig. 136. Fastening the triangles.

XVI. Stitch the welt into position.

A. The welt may be machine-stitched around the top and sides.

B. You may hand-stitch 1/16 in. on the right side of the coat below the welt seam. Another method is to machine-stitch from the right side directly in the groove of the coat-welt seam. Do not go through the pouch lining.

C. Use the invisible tack or over-and-over stitch on the corners and the slanting back stitch on the ends of the welt from the wrong side. Or slip-stitch the ends of the welt to the coat.

XVII. Press.

A. Attach the stay. See Figure 125, p. 63.
B. Hard-press on the wrong side first.
C. Off-press on the right side.

Slash-Bound Pocket (Slot or Set-in Bound)

There are many variations of this type of pocket: It may have a curved or straight mouthline, wide or narrow binding strips finishing the edge of the mouthline, variations in the fabric binding, and modifications in the direction in which the seam edges are turned at the mouthline.

Generally, the pocketline for a man's breast pocket should be on line with the bottom pocket and the lowest corner on line with the armhole.

I. Mark the mouthline.

A. Mark with contrasting basting thread the line indicated by the pattern, which was altered if necessary during the first fitting.

B. Extend the markings 1 in. beyond the end of the mouthline and guide-baste at each end at right angles to it (Fig. 137).

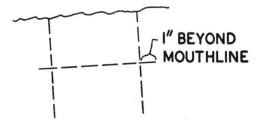

I″ BEYOND MOUTHLINE

Fig. 137. Marking the mouthline.

C. The average breast pocket is 4¼ to 5⅝ in. long.

II. Cut the binding strips.

A. Cut two strips of wool 2 to 3 in. wide and 2 in. longer than the finished mouthline.

B. If the pocket is straight, these may be cut either warpwise, fillingwise, or on the bias.

C. A curved pocket must have the strips cut on the true bias.

D. You may want to match plaids or patterned fabrics.

III. Cut the pocket-pouch strip.

A. Cut the pocket-pouch strip of silesia, wigan, lining, or muslin.

B. In a fairly straight pocket, cut just one strip. Generally, two pieces are used.

C. Cut the pouch 1 to 2 in. wider than the mouthline and as deep as desired. Be sure the warplines of the pieces are parallel to the warpline of the body of the coat. The shape of the pouch depends on the location of the pocket (Fig. 138).

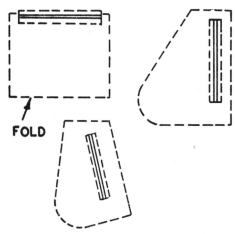

FOLD

Fig. 138.   Shapes of pouches.

IV. Cut the facing strip.

A. Cut of wool fabric 2 in. wide and 1 in. longer than mouthline. It is desirable to have one length on a selvage.

B. The upper edge should be congruent with the pocket pouch according to the slant of the pocket.

V. Cut the pocket stay.

A. Cut of muslin or wigan 1½ to 2 in. wide and 2 in. longer than the mouthline.

B. See that the warp runs lengthwise of strip.

VI. Apply the pocket stay.

A. Place the center of the stay on the mouthline on the wrong side of the garment.

B. Baste into position.

VII. Baste the binding strips into position.

A. Place the binding strips, right side against the right side of the coat. One falls above the mouthline and the other below the mouthline. One edge of each strip meets at the mouthline (Fig. 139).

B. Baste into position.

C. Mark the ends of the mouthline on the binding strip (Fig. 139).

BINDING STRIPS

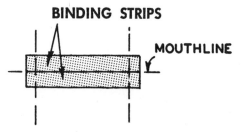

MOUTHLINE

Fig. 139.   Marking the mouthline for the binding strip.

VIII. Stitch the binding strips.

A. Stitch a ⅛- to ¼-in. seam from the mouthline on each binding strip, ending on the marked ends.

B. You may stitch ³⁄₁₆ in. for a heavier fabric. A ⅛-in. seam gives a piped effect while a ¼-in. seam a bound effect.

C. Fasten the ends securely by tying or retracing the stitching at ends.

IX. Cut pocket mouthline.

A. Cut through the coat and stay on the mouthline to ⅜ in. from the ends (Fig. 140).

B. Cut diagonally to the ends of the stitching line, slightly curving the diagonal. This will form a triangle at each end (Fig. 140).

Fig. 140.   Cut the pocket mouthline.

X. Press the mouthline-binding seams.

A. For a flat appearance, press the seams open.

B. For a bound effect, the seam edges may be pressed toward the mouth-line.

C. For a piped effect, the seam edges are turned away from the mouthline.

D. A strip of tape may be placed along the inside of the fold of the binding strip to keep the pocket from stretch-ing. It may be fastened at the ends to the stay, the coat facing, and the side seam.

XI. Finish the mouthline.

A. Pull the binding strips through the opening to the wrong side.

B. Roll the lower binding to the desired width (⅛ to ¼ in.). Pull it snugly over the seam making it a little nar-rower over the dart seam.

C. Baste with small stitches.

D. Stitch from the right side directly on the groove of the seam on the lower binding.

E. Baste the upper binding snugly over the seam and baste. This should be the same width as the lower bind-ing. *Do not stitch.*

F. Diagonal-baste the mouthline edges together on the right side.

G. Press.

XII. Prepare the under-pocket pouch.

A. Place the facing strip on one end of the pouch with the right sides of both up, matching the raw edges. The wrong side of the facing is against the right side of the pouch (Fig. 141).

B. Stitch along the selvage (Fig. 141).

C. If a selvage is not available, turn under the wool and stitch.

D. The wool and the lining may be edge-stitched together close to the top edge.

XIII. Attach the pocket pouch.

A. Attach the single edge (if a strip) of the pouch to the lower binding edge, right sides together. Stitch.

B. If two pocket-pouch pieces are used, attach the top edge of the upper pocket pouch to the lower binding edge, right sides together. Stitch.

C. The seam may be pressed down if lining material and lightweight wool are used, but if it is bulky, press open.

D. Fold the under-pocket pouch into position ½ in. or more above the mouthline. The wool facing falls over the pocket opening. Baste into posi-tion.

E. From the right side, stitch through *all* thicknesses in the groove of the top binding-mouthline seam as at the bottom.

XIV. Close the pocket pouch.

A. Fold the end of the pocket and stay so that the right sides are together and so that the triangle and pocket linings extend outward (Fig. 142).

B. Stitch up, down to the bottom, across the bottom, up the other side, through the other triangular piece. Stitching upward on the triangle

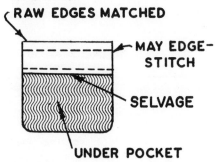

RAW EDGES MATCHED

MAY EDGE-STITCH

SELVAGE

UNDER POCKET

Fig. 141. The under-pocket pouch.

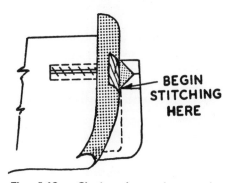

BEGIN STITCHING HERE

Fig. 142. Closing the pocket pouch.

keeps the pocket from spreading (Fig. 142).

C. The side lines may slant outward for men's pockets.

XV. Press.

A. Attach the stay. See Fig. 125, p. 63.

B. Hard-press first from the wrong side.

C. Off-press from the right side.

NOTE: The pocket-pouch linings may be attached to binding strips before the strips are attached to the pocket mouthline. To make a corded pocket, the binding strips are tucked and strands of yarn or heavy string are drawn through it to form a corded piping.

Patch Pocket

Patch pockets are more satisfactory from the standpoint of design and durability for many types of tailored garments. They are of various sizes and shapes, depending on their location and the design of the garment. Patch pockets are lined on most tailored garments. Some unlined jackets or summer suits may have unlined patch pockets.

I. Mark the pocket position.

A. Mark the pocket position in a desirable location according to the figure and the style of the garment (Fig. 143).

Fig. 143. Marking for the pocket.

B. Mark the outline with contrasting basting thread.

II. Cut the pocket and mark the seamline.

A. The pocket pattern from the garment pattern may be used.

B. The larger the figure, the larger the pockets and vice versa.

C. A man's side pocket measures 6¾ to 7½ in. by 8 in., a breast pocket 4¾ to 5½ in. by 5½ to 6 in. Often there are flaps above a patch pocket.

D. Cut the pocket of wool the desired shape plus a ½-in. seam allowance on three sides and a 1-in. hem at the top. It should match the grain and pattern of the garment area unless cut for contrast (Fig. 144).

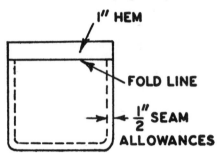

Fig. 144. Cutting the pocket.

E. Mark the seamline and the foldline with basting or tracing carbon.

III. Cut the lining.

A. Cut the lining on the same grain as the pocket, only 1 in. shorter in length.

B. Mark the seamline and the foldline with basting or tracing carbon.

IV. Apply the stay tape.

A. Tape the lower edge of the hem on the wrong side, just above the foldline with preshrunk tape to prevent stretching. Machine-stitch in place Fig. 145, a); or

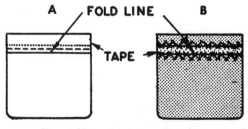

Fig. 145. Applying the stay.

B. Tape the upper edge of the patch pocket by placing the upper edge of the tape against the foldline of hem. Catch-stitch both edges lightly to the pocket (Fig. 145, b).

C. Sometimes the entire pocket is reinforced.

V. Join the lining to the hem.

A. Place the right side of the pocket (hem end) against the right side of the lining.

B. Stitch a ¼-in. seam. Press (Fig. 146).

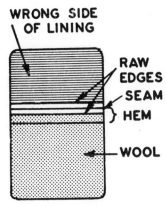

Fig. 146.   Joining lining and hem.

VI. **Apply lining to pocket (A–I — machine method).**

A. Place the wool pocket and the lining right sides together, the wool side uppermost.

B. Pin at the centers and corners.

C. Push back the wool ⅟₁₆ in. from the edge of the facing evenly around pocket. This allows the seamline to turn to the underside; or

D. Tailor-baste about 1 in. from the raw edge of the lining and the pocket. Ease the wool between the tailor basting and the edge. Baste again on the seamline (Fig. 147A).

E. Machine-stitch with the lining uppermost, leaving an opening through which to turn the pocket.

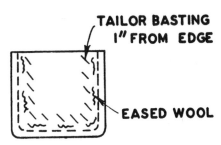

Fig. 147A.   Basting the wool.

F. Press open the seam allowances. Trim the seam to ⅛ in. and cut out the bulk at the outward curve or corner (Fig. 147B).

Fig. 147B.   Making the corner.

G. Turn the pocket right side out through the opening.

H. Finger-press the turned edges so that the seamline rolls under toward the lining. Baste around the edge.

I. Close the opening by hand. Press.

Hand method (J–L):

J. After the lining is attached at the hem, place the lining into position with the wrong side of the lining against the wrong side of the wool.

K. As a guide for turning under the seam allowance machine-baste about ⅟₁₆ in. around the sides and lower edge, outside the marked seamline (Fig. 148). Baste under the seam allowance. Cut out the excess at the corners and rounded edges. Miter at the top corners. Press. Trim the seam to slightly less than ¼ in. (raw edge) with catch stitching. Press.

L. *Optional:* Fasten the seam allowance

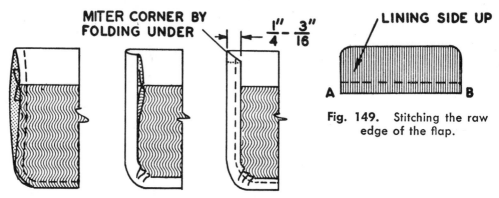

MITER CORNER BY FOLDING UNDER

$\frac{1''}{4} - \frac{3''}{16}$

LINING SIDE UP

A   B

Fig. 149. Stitching the raw edge of the flap.

Fig. 148. Applying the lining by hand.

VII. Attach the pocket to the garment.

A. Place the pocket on the marked position. Pin it so that it will curve smoothly and will not lie too tightly against the garment.

B. Tailor-baste through the center. Then baste the outer edges to the garment.

C. Fasten the pocket to the coat.

    1. *Machine method:* You may top-stitch about ¼ to ½ in. from the edge around three sides of the pocket. Reinforce the corners on the wrong side of the coat with invisible tacks. As a guide for top-stitching, you may make a pattern of paper and pin or baste it to the pocket and stitch close to the edge of the pattern.

    2. *Hand-stitch method:* Hand-stitch from the wrong side of the garment along the three sides. Reinforce the corners with over-and-over stitching or invisible tacks. Hand-stitch close to the edge beginning at the upper left-hand corner (from the wrong side) with a slanting backstitch. Do a second

row of stitching ⅜ in. on the inside of the first row.

D. To reinforce the top corners, you may place linen tape or a strip of wigan 2 in. wide and the length of the pocket, to a side seam, underneath the top edge of the pocket on the wrong side of the garment. The stitching at the corner of the pocket attaches this reinforcement. The other end is caught in the seam.

Flap

I. Prepare the flap.

Prepare the flap in the same manner as the lined pocket; *however,* leave the top edge open.

II. **Attach the flap to the coat.**

A. Stitch above the raw edge of the flap from A to B (Fig. 149).

B. Turn the flap down and make a ¼-in. finished seam across the top. This covers the raw edges.

C. Sometimes on dressmaker suits, the raw edges are turned under and slip-stitched together and hand-stitched to the coat.

CHAPTER **15**

Shaping the Garment and the Interfacing

THE wool garment and interfacing (canvas) are shaped before the pockets are constructed, and before they are attached to each other. Shaping is done so the garment fits over natural curves of the body, as at the bust, waistline, underarm, and hipline (see Chapter 8, p. 38, for hints on pressing, shaping, and the use of a press cloth).

Shaping the Garment

I. Shape at the end of the shoulder dart.
A. Place the end of the dart over the rounded part of the cushion, wrong side up.
B. Sponge lightly and press.

II. Shape for the ball and socket joint.
A. This procedure stretches the material making provision for a ball and socket joint.
B. Place the two fronts, right sides together, repeating the following operations, or shape each front separately.
C. Place the iron at A in Figure 150 at the gorge and using the side edge of the iron for stretching, work with a circular motion from right to left. Keep the tip of the iron at a central point.
D. Beginning at B reverse the circular motion. This will cause a slight bulge from the joint.
E. Be careful not to overstretch.

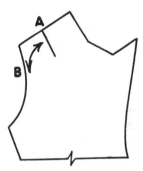

Fig. 150. Shaping the ball and socket joint.

III. Shrink for the hollow of the shoulders.
A. Place the middle of the shoulder on the middle of the board.
B. Place the point of the iron on or near the shoulder seam allowance.
C. Shrink in fullness for the hollow by easing the material under the iron with the left hand while pressing.

Fig. 151. Shrinking for the shoulder hollow.

Tip the iron to one side as easing is done to avoid stretching (Fig. 151).

IV. Shape the front lower amscye.

A. Remove the tape from the lower armscye, from the notch to the seamline.

B. Run a fine basting stitch along the seamline from the notch to the seam. Draw it up about ⅜ in. Fasten the thread.

C. Place the armscye along the curved edge of the cheese block.

D. Press down on the area to remove the fullness, lifting the iron to avoid creases.

E. After the fullness is removed, snip and take out the bastings, replacing the tape.

F. Some tailors use a drawing-in stitch on the underarm which remains in the garment. Merely shrink in the fullness.

V. Shape for the hip.

A. Place the garment so that the fullness below the waistline dart may be shrunk out.

B. Place the point of the iron on the lower part of the waistline dart.

C. Press semicircularly across the end of the dart (Fig. 152).

D. Do not stretch the lower hip.

Fig. 152. Shaping the hip.

VI. Shape the garment for the bust.

A. Place the flat side of the cheese block toward you.

B. Place both coat fronts up to the figure in position, and chalk-mark the tips of the bust.

C. Place the highest point 1 of the bust over the curved edge of the cheese block (Fig. 153). You will observe

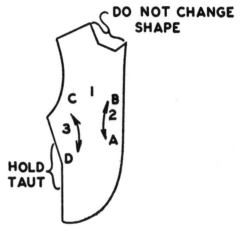

Fig. 153. Shaping for the bust.

fullness at 2. Shrink out this fullness by dampening with a sponge and shrinking with a circular motion of the iron. Work from A to B gradually moving toward the front edge of the garment.

D. Turn the garment over so that 1 is again over the curved edge of the cheese block and the fullness at 3 is on the cheese board. Shrink out this fullness (C to D, Fig. 153).

E. Place padding under the shaped bust area and allow it to dry.

F. Use a tailor's ham if a cheese block is not available.

VII. Other shaping.

A. Shape the ends of all the darts by placing each over the rounded part of the cushion. Sponge lightly on the wrong side. Press.

B. Shape the back armscye as the front armscye, drawing in only ¼ in.

C. On fitted jackets, use a drawstring to remove fullness at the waistline curve, both front and back, as at the armscye.

D. Shape the back for a prominent shoulder blade. Mark and shape as for the ball and socket and hollow shoulder.

E. For shaping the sleeve, see Chapter 25, pp. 102–103.

VIII. Shape the interfacing.

A. After the construction of the interfacing, steam-press and shape it to fit the body curves the same as the body of the coat.

B. Allow it to dry before attaching it to the garment.

CHAPTER 16

Attaching the Interfacing to the Coat

I. Apply the interfacing to the coat front.

A. Place the coat front on top of the canvas.

    1. Put the canvas on a dress form, placing the wool on top, or put the canvas over a ham on a table with the wool coat front on top.

    2. If the latter method is used, put the fingers of the left hand under the shaped areas such as the hip and bust sections.

B. Baste the canvas to the coat front.

    1. Beginning with the right side of the right forepart, 3 to 4 in. down from the shoulder, tailor-baste from A to B, Figure 154. There may be some fullness pushing toward the center front.

    2. Baste from C, the point of the neck hollow, to the creaseline continuing to the top button D, extending down the coat front to E (Fig. 154).

    3. From D to E, Figure 154, place the outer edge of the garment over the edge of the table when tailor-basting. This eases in the fullness so the garment will roll in slightly at the bottom.

    4. Baste the left forepart from the bottom up.

    5. Additional rows of basting may be done from F to G and from H to I. Always remain at least 3 in. from the seams. These bastings remain in the garment until the final pressing.

    6. On a man's sport coat, the basting may follow the diagram (Fig. 155).

       NOTE: If the garment is buttoned to the neck and does not have a lapel, baste the entire canvas to the coat in the front.

       If the facing is cut onto the garment, baste the interfacing to the coat-facing fold line.

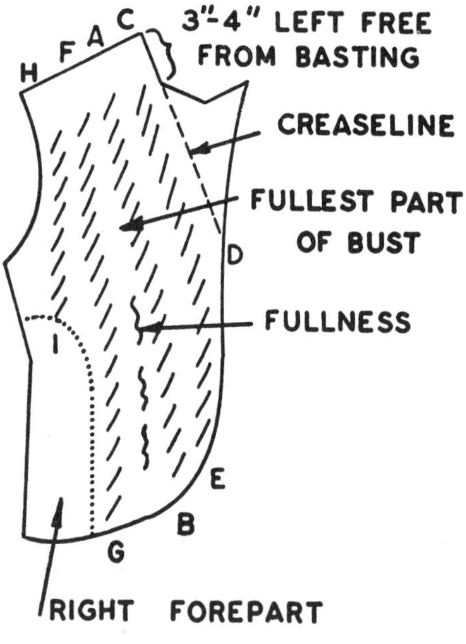

II. Apply the interfacing to the coat back.

A. Place the coat back on top of the canvas.

    1. Follow the same procedure as with the coat front.

Fig. 154. Applying the interfacing to the coat front.

2. Do two to three rows of diagonal basting on each side (left and right) of the center back, working from the center back toward the sleeve edge (Fig. 156).

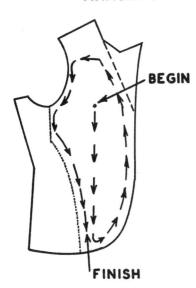

BEGIN

FINISH

Fig. 155. Basting a man's
sport coat.

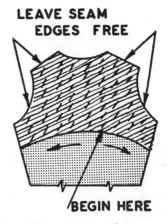

**LEAVE SEAM
EDGES FREE**

BEGIN HERE

Fig. 156. Basting the canvas
to the coat back.

2. Adjust and pin the interfacing to the coat center back.
B. Baste the canvas to the coat back.
   1. Diagonal-baste down the center back. If the garment has a center back seam, this could be basted permanently from the canvas side (Fig. 156).

3. Leave the seam edges free, with the bastings about 1½ in. from the cut edge.

III. Attach the cotton felt, if desired (see pp. 52–53).

CHAPTER **17**

Pad-Stitching the Lapel and Taping the Creaseline*

I. Pad-stitch the lapel.

A. Mark the breakline (creaseline). This line was established during the first fitting. Baste with contrasting thread.

B. Pad-stitch the inside of the breakline.
1. See Chapter 8, p. 36, for the pad-stitching procedure.
2. Use silk thread matched to the wool and no knot.
3. Pad-stitch one or two rows parallel to the breakline, beginning 1 in. behind the breakline at the neck edge, stopping 3 in. short of the coat edge at the bottom of the creaseline (Fig. 157). (Some tailors omit this pad-stitching.)

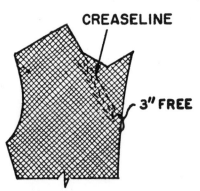

Fig. 157. Pad-stitching.

C. Pad-stitch the lapel.
1. Hold the lapel in the left hand so that it rolls back on the garment as it will on the wearer, thumb on top, index finger underneath the lapel.
2. On the canvas side, make parallel rows of pad-stitching beginning ¼–½ in. inside of the creaseline at the neck edge on down. Then return up to the top continuing down and up out to the lapel point. Do not turn the garment around.
3. Shape the lapel with your fingers, rolling it, pulling your thumbs on the canvas, toward one, and pushing and easing with the index finger. Provide little ease for a flat lapel.
4. Leave the seam edges, plus ⅛ in. free along the seamline of the lapel (Fig. 158).

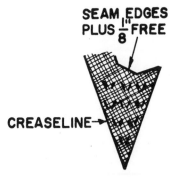

Fig. 158. Allow ⅛ in. free along the seamline.

---

* Omit this procedure if the garment does not have a revers lapel.

5. Do the right lapel from the neck edge to the top button. Reverse the procedure for the left lapel.

II. Tape the creaseline.

A. Cut the tape for the breakline.
   1. Cut a strip of tape the length of the creaseline plus 2½ in. to carry onto the collar seam.
   2. Be sure the tape is thoroughly shrunk.

B. Pin at right angles and baste on the tape.
   1. The tape may be placed with one edge on the breakline, the other edge toward the body of the coat or pinned and basted ½ in. beyond the breakline. This keeps the bias creaseline from stretching and holds the coat close to the body over the bustline (Fig. 159).
   2. Keep the tape snug. Hold the coat against yourself and adjust the tape.
      a) For a full bust, ease in the lapel more.
      b) For a flat chest, ease in slightly.

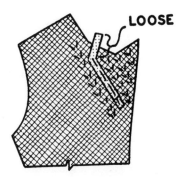

Fig. 159.   Taping the creaseline.

   c) Shorten, where it crosses the bustline, to keep the coat close to the figure.
   d) On a man's sport coat, draw in about ½ in. Some tailors are able to draw this in about ¾ in.
   3. Allow the loose end of the tape to extend about 1½ in. above the breakline (Fig. 159).

C. Fell the bridle tape.
   1. Using matching silk thread, fell both edges of the tape to the reinforcement.
   2. Use medium-sized stitches.

CHAPTER **18**

Trimming the Interfacing and Taping the Front Edges

I. Trim the interfacing.

A. Check the shape of the lapel.

1. Pad-stitching and taping may change the shape slightly.
2. Use the pattern to check both sides to see that they are identical, or cut a cardboard shaper to remark the edges of the lapel.
3. The shaper is the lapel minus the seam allowances.

B. Trim the interfacing from the coat front edges.

1. Trim the interfacing seam allowance plus ⅛ in. (Fig. 160).
2. Trim from the bottom of the hem to the tip of the lapel, and across the top of the lapel to the collar notch. *Do not* trim the gorgeline (Fig. 160).

II. Tape the front edges.

A. Pin and baste on the tape.

1. Place the jacket on the table with the interfacing side up.
2. Use shrunken ⅜-in. linen tape or selvages.

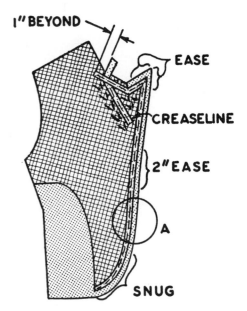

TRIM AWAY SEAM
ALLOWANCE PLUS $\frac{1}{8}$ "

Fig. 160. Trimming the interfacing.

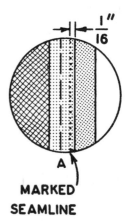

MARKED
SEAMLINE

Fig. 161. Taping the front edges.

3. Begin by placing the tape *1 in. beyond the creaseline* at the neckline, across the top of the lapel, down the front edge, around the bottom to the inner edge of the facing.
4. Pin so that the outer edge of the tape extends ⅟₁₆ in. beyond the seamline, toward the cut edge (Fig. 161, a).
5. Use a cardboard shaper while pinning around the lapel. Skip steps 6 and 7, if no lapel is required.
6. Ease the tape for 1½ in. at the front edge at the point of the lapel and at the top buttonhole for 2 in. (Fig. 161).
7. At a point 1 in. above the top buttonhole to 3 in. from a point above the buttonhole, keep the tape snug for the desired amount of roll in the lapel (Fig. 161).
8. Baste with fine running stitches through the middle of the tape.
9. Clip or notch the inside edge of the tape where necessary to make it lie flat or shape with an iron. Carefully miter the tape at the corners if the lapel is pointed. For a curved lapel, notch the tape in several places and shape it. You may cut out excess bulk (Fig. 162, a and b).
10. Check both lapels again to be sure they are identical.

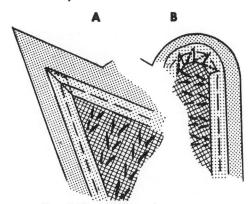

Fig. 162. Taping the corners.

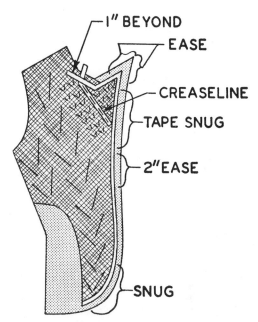

Fig. 163. Taping the front edges.

B. Fell the tape.
  1. Fell the inside edge of the tape to the interfacing only, using a felling stitch. The other edge of the tape (close to the cut edge of the garment front) will be stitched with the facing and the garment seam.
  2. Use thread to match the wool.
  3. Both edges of the tape may be hemmed by hand, if the tape is not stitched into the seam. The outer edge is hemmed to the stitching line.
  4. Sometimes, if the reinforcement is lightweight, the interfacing is trimmed away after the tape is stitched on. This is a faster method but not as effective as the preferred method described above.

III. **Pad-stitch the remainder of the canvas (Fig. 163).**

  Pad-stitch the remainder of the front canvas area with loose, large pad stitches *if* the stitches do not show on the right side; otherwise, omit.

CHAPTER 19

Preparing a Tailored Buttonhole

(Two-Strip Method)

TAILORED (piped) or corded button-holes are not only used as a means of fastening but also as a means of decoration. In construction, they are similar to slashed and bound pockets. Make a practice buttonhole (IV, D).

I. **Mark the placement of the button-hole.**

A. Be sure the center front of the coat is marked with colored thread.

B. Since buttons slide toward the outer end of a buttonhole when a coat is worn, the buttonhole extends beyond the center front toward the front of garment.

C. Use the pattern to guide placement. (Step II, A to D, may be done at this time if one is experienced in tailoring and certain of buttonhole placement.)

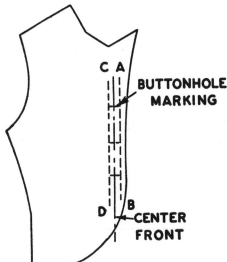

Fig. 165.   Marking the buttonholes.

D. Machine-baste or hand-baste a guide-line with long stitches on the jacket front the entire length of the button-hole sections, from A to B, Figure 165. This vertical row is ⅛ in. from the center front line toward the fabric edge *unless the pattern indicates otherwise.*

E. Determine the length of the button-hole by measuring the diameter of the button plus one thickness of the button.

F. After determining the length of the buttonhole, measure over the desired amount from A to B and make another vertical row C–D, Figure 165. These two parallel lines mark the ends of the buttonhole.

G. Mark the locations of each button-hole, using a small machine stitch, between two markings. This stitch-ing must be on the straight of the goods with matching thread (Fig. 166).

H. Mark by machine-basting or hand-basting ¼ in. above and ¼ in. below

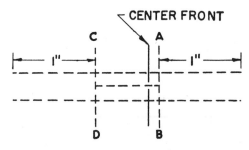

Fig. 166.   Detail of the position of the buttonhole.

the location line. Extend 1 in. beyond the vertical lines (Fig. 166).

II. Prepare the coat for buttonholes.

A. Using a sharp pointed scissors, cut out a rectangle from the canvas (interfacing) the length of the buttonhole plus ¼ in. and ¾ in. wide. Be careful not to remove the buttonhole guidelines.

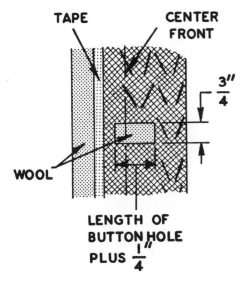

Fig. 167. Preparing the coat.

B. Place a reinforcement of wigan or silesia so it extends ¼ in. over the opening. Iron-on tape may be substituted for loosely woven materials.

C. Catch-stitch or fell the wigan to the canvas.

D. Buttonholes will be made through the reinforcement.

III. Cut the binding strips.

A. Cut a strip of garment material on the grain (lengthwise usually), 1¼ in. wide and twice the length of the buttonhole plus 2 in. for each buttonhole. You may pull the threads to insure a true grain.

B. Buttonhole strips of plaids and stripes must match the pattern in the garment or be made on a true

bias. For a corded buttonhole stitch yarn into a bias strip.

IV. Prepare the buttonhole strips.

A. Fold the strip in half lengthwise, wrong sides together. Pin.

B. Stitch ⅛ in. from the folded edge. This distance may vary. See step D, below.

C. For a corded effect, you may pull yarn through the tucks after stitching, or place cording in the strip and stitch over it.

D. For lighter weight materials the stitching on the strip may be 3/16 in. from the edge. On heavy coat materials with heavy cording, the strips may be stitched ¼ in. from the folded edge. In these cases, the guidelines in step I, H, will have to be varied. They should be twice the width of the finished strip above the marked line and below the marked line.

E. Trim off one seam extension to ¼ in. from the stitching line (Fig. 168).

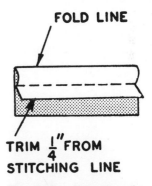

FOLD LINE

TRIM ¼" FROM
STITCHING LINE

Fig. 168. Trimming the buttonhole strip.

V. Attach the strip to the garment.

A. Cut the strips into pieces the length of each buttonhole plus 1 in. There will be two strips for each buttonhole.

B. On the right side of the coat, place the folded edge of the strip on the

basted line ¼ in. above the buttonhole marking, trimmed seam up.

C. Baste, stitch on machine basting on
the strip, retracing as shown, ending
exactly on the parallel vertical markings (Fig. 169).

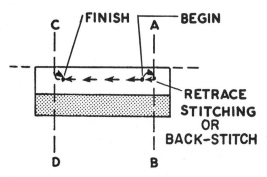

Fig. 169.   Attaching the top strip to
the garment.

D. Repeat with the second strip, placing
the folded edge on the lower basted
line ¼ in. below the buttonhole
marking. Baste and stitch, retracing
as shown. Be careful not to catch in
the first tucked strip.

E. Check from the wrong side of the
garment. The permanent stitching
lines must be straight and parallel
⅛ in. on each side of the guidelines.

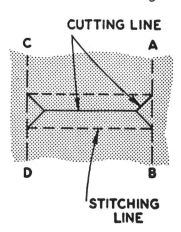

Fig. 170.   Slashing the
bottonhole.

VI. **Slash the buttonhole.**

A. Cut the buttonhole from the wrong
side on the marked buttonhole line
to ⅜ in. from the end. Keep the
edges of the strips apart on the right
side with the fingers (Fig. 170).

B. Clip diagonally to the permanent
stitching at the corners, *not* through
it.

C. This leaves a triangle at each end.

VII. **Turn the buttonhole.**

A. Pull the tucked strips through to the
wrong side.

B. Pull into shape and diagonal-baste
the folded edges from the right side.

VIII. **Finish the buttonhole.**

A. Fold back the garment at the end of
the buttonhole, right sides together,
exposing the triangle.

B. Stitch across the ends of the strip
and the triangle. Backstitch (Fig.
171).

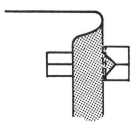

Fig. 171.   Finishing
the buttonhole.

C. Repeat this process on the other end
of the buttonhole.

IX. **Apply facing to the buttonhole.**

A. This is done after the facing is attached to the garment.

B. Fold the facing into position. From
the buttonhole side, place a pin in
the opening at cach end of the buttonhole (Fig. 172, a).

C. From the facing side, baste a line
from one pin to the other (Fig. 172,
b).

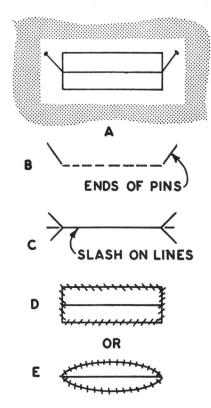

Fig. 172.   Applying facing to
the bottonhole.

D. Cut the same as for the buttonhole
(Fig. 172, c).

E. Turn under each side and the ends,
and fell the facing to the buttonhole.
Take an extra stitch at the corners
(Fig. 172, d); or

F. Cut a straight line and fold back the
facing to form an oval. There are no
corners with this method, and it
should not be used at the top button of a convertible neckline (Fig.
172, e).

Simplified Tailored Buttonhole
(One-Strip Method)

I. Mark the placement of the buttonhole.

A. See step I, A through G, of the preceding procedure.

B. Baste-stitch a line ¼ in. above the
buttonhole line.

II. Prepare the coat for the buttonhole.
See the preceding procedure, step
II, A to D.

III. Prepare the buttonhole strips.

A. Cut a lengthwise strip 2½ in. wide
and twice the length of total number of buttonholes.

B. Cut a 2½-in. strip of lined paper
with ½-in. spaces the same length.

C. Match the edges of the paper and
the fabric and baste-stitch on the
lines of the paper, two lines ½ in.
apart, the length of the strips (Fig.
173).

D. Remove the paper from the stitched
strip.

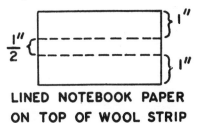

LINED NOTEBOOK PAPER
ON TOP OF WOOL STRIP
Fig. 173.   One-strip method.

IV. Attach the strip to the garment.

A. Cut the strip into pieces twice the
length of each buttonhole or the buttonhole length plus 1 in.

B. Fold the strip on the baste-stitched
line and place the fold on the basting

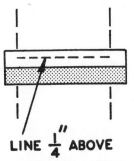

LINE ¼" ABOVE
BUTTONHOLE MARKINGS
Fig. 174.   Attaching the strip.

line which is ¼ in. above the button-hole line, with equal amounts on each side of the buttonhole. Be sure the right side of the strip is against the right side of the garment (Fig. 174). (You may trim to ⅛ in. from the stitching line on one seam.)

C. With permanent machine-stitching, stitch ⅛ in. from the folded edge between the vertical parallel markings. Fasten the thread at the ends.

D. Fold the strip on the second baste-stitch line and repeat the stitching, being careful not to catch the upper end of strip.

E. On the wrong side the lines of stitching must be ¼ in. apart, straight, and parallel.

V. **Slash, turn, and finish.**

See steps VI, VII, VIII, and IX of the above procedure.

NOTE: Rencrest and Dritz make an inexpensive buttonhole binder which makes either a welt or corded button-hole.

CHAPTER **20**

Constructing Side and Shoulder Seams

FOR the most part, the seams in coats and suits are not treated any differently from the way they are in making garments of wool in dressmaking.

I. Shoulder seam.

A. Design the seam.

1. In tailoring, the shoulder seam is usually curved at the neckline so that the shoulder will curve up onto the neck (Fig. 177).

Fig. 177. Curve for the shoulder seam.

2. This curve should be less than ¼ in.

B. Baste the seams together.

1. Baste the shoulder seam from the neck to the tip of shoulder, easing the back part onto the forepart.
2. See Chapter 9, p. 45, for instructions for handling tape in basting.

C. Stitch the seam.

1. Stitch the seam using directional stitching from the neck to the shoulder.
2. Do not catch the tape in the seam if the fabric is bulky and firm. Remove the tape.

3. If the fabric is loosely woven or stretchy, stitch the tape in the seam.

D. Press the seam.

Press the curved seam slightly open on a tailor's ham.

II. Side seam.

A. Stitch the seam.

Use directional stitching (stitch from the highest to the lowest part or from the widest to the narrowest part).

B. Press the seam.

The vertical body seams are usually pressed open unless indicated otherwise by the pattern.

C. Finish the seam.

1. If seams are very curved they may be treated so they will lie flat.

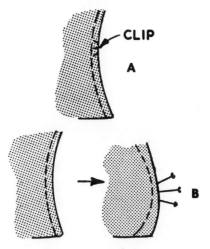

Fig. 178. Making the side seam lie flat.

a. Clip toward the seam (Fig. 178, a); or

b. Stretch the inward curve outward with the iron on curves that are not too pronounced. Stretch the seam, pin to the board, dampen, and press (Fig. 178, b).

2. Seams on lined suits and coats are never finished unless the material ravels excessively. Such seams may be overcasted loosely so that the edges are not drawn.

Attaching Interfacing at Seamlines

I. Lap the interfacing on top of the wool seamline at the shoulder and side seam.

A. Trim off the excess seam.

B. Pin the interfacing into position.

II. Catch-stitch the interfacing to the wool seam (Fig. 179).

A. Attach the interfacing along the seamline, being careful not to go through to the right side of the garment.

B. Use thread to match the wool.

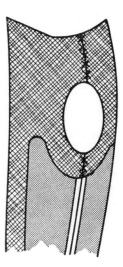

Fig. 179. Attaching interfacing at the seamline.

CHAPTER **21**

Applying the Front Facing

I. Lay the facing smoothly on top of the coat.

A. Put the right sides together with the facing over the coat.

B. If the facing has more neckline curve than the coat, hold it even at the neckline and also at the lower jacket front.

C. The lapel facing, which has an extra allowance beyond the shaped cut edge, extends beyond the coat lapel to allow for the lapel roll.

II. Baste the facing into position.

A. Baste down the breakline and continue down the coat front, beginning at A, Figure 181, about 4 in. from the shoulder.

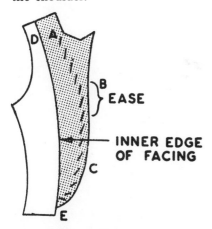

Fig. 181. Basting the facing
into position.

B. At B, Figure 181, in the region of the top buttonhole, push in the slight fullness on the facing for a space of 2 in. so as to allow for lapel roll at the bottom of the breakline.

C. Baste about 1 in. from the cut edge.

D. Hold the facing tight around the curve at the bottom of the jacket between C and E, Figure 181. From the top button, B, to the bottom of the coat, E, hold the seamline over the edge of the table in order that the coat rolls toward the facing when finished.

E. With the facing side up, baste along the inner edge of the facing from D to E or on the facing-lining seam if the lining was attached (Fig. 181).

III. Baste the lapel facing.

A. Lay the coat back along the breakline over your hand with the wrong side of the facing up.

B. Baste with diagonal basting beginning at the breakline, running parallel to it.

C. Ease the fullness with your fingers, making several rows of diagonal basting stitches until you reach the point of the lapel (Fig. 182). The figure shows the left lapel. Reverse the procedure for the right lapel.

D. The fullness should lie parallel to

Fig. 182. Putting fullness
in the lapel.

89

the breakline. The corner of the lapel should have a decided roll.

NOTE: The amount of roll should be determined by the weight of the fabric and the figure:

1. The heavier the fabric, the more the fabric should be eased in.
2. A high roll should be worn by flat-chested women.

E. Another method is to baste the creaseline. Then take a ¼-in. tuck tapering to nothing at either end about ¼ in. from the creaseline. Baste the outer seam edge. Remove the pins to check the bulge in the facing for roll before stitching (Fig. 183).

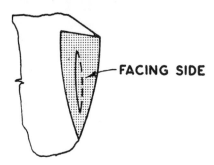

Fig. 183.   Basting the creaseline.

IV. Stitch the facing to position.

A. Stitch from the coat side, with the interfacing on top. On the right forepart stitch from the bottom up and reverse for the left.

B. Stitch ¹⁄₁₆ in. on the edge of the

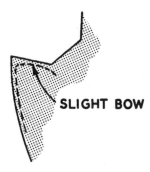

Fig. 184.   Stitching the top of the lapel.

stay tape. Do not catch the interfacing.

C. When stitching the top of the lapel, stitch with a slight bow to insure a straight edge when turned (Fig. 184).

D. At the point, stitch one stitch across the end to make a point. The stitch may be shortened slightly at the point.

V. Press the edge seam.

A. After the bastings are removed, press the seams open on the edge presser.

B. Press the seams toward the corners, using moisture.

C. Trim the coat seam to ⅜ to ¼ in., and the facing seam slightly shorter, ¼ to ⅛ in. Reverse the procedure for the lapel beginning at the top button to keep the facing coat seam from rolling (Fig. 185A). Trim off

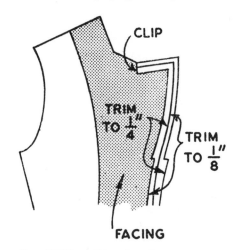

Fig. 185A.   Trimming the coat seam

the excess at the point of the lapel by removing a triangle. Trim the remaining corners (Fig. 185B).

D. Fell the trimmed seam to the interfacing under the facing or see step VI, D, below. Use a running catch stitch (Fig. 185C).

VI. Turn the facing back and baste the edges.

APPLYING THE FRONT FACING

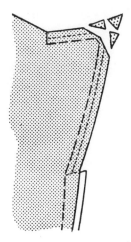

Fig. 185B. Trimming the
excess at the point
of the lapel.

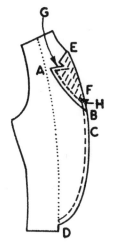

Fig. 186. Rolling
the lapel seams.

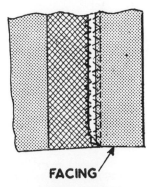

FACING

Fig. 185C. Felling the
trimmed seam to
the interfacing.

A. Baste close to the edge using. fine stitches. Take a backstitch about every four to five stitches.

B. Roll the lapel seam toward the coat, A to B, Figure 186. Roll the remainder of the seam toward the facing C to D.

C. Tailor-baste the lapel, rolled back with two rows of basting — one near the creaseline (E to F, Fig. 186) and one near the center of the lapel (G to H, Fig. 186).

D. Optional: If step V, D, is not done, the facing may be tacked to the interfacing to keep the facing from

rolling toward the front. Stitches should be long and loose.

VII. **Baste the lining in position (if the lining is stitched).**

A. Permanent-baste the lining seam to the interfacing from A to B, Figure 187, turning the lining back and attaching the seam to the canvas.

B. Baste the lining in position, remaining approximately 3 to 4 in. from the seamline (Fig. 187).

C. Pat up the fullness at C before basting the side seam and the bottom to allow for the hip (Fig. 187).

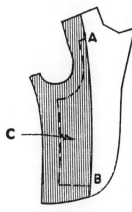

Fig. 187. Basting the
lining in position.

CHAPTER 22

Preparing and Attaching an Undercollar

(Felled or Machine-Stitched to the Neckline)

A MARK of good tailoring is evidenced in the design, shaping, fitting, and hand-stitched application of the collar. Current styles, however, affect the design of the collars for women's garments so that many times a strictly hard man-tailored collar may not be desirable.

The methods of attaching collars are many. The undercollar may be of melton or self-material and attached by felling or machine-stitching. The uppercollar may be attached by hand- or machine-stitching. Sometimes it is desirable to complete the collar before it is attached. Then there is a simplified short-cut method of applying the collar to a garment for the beginner with little knowledge of tailoring. Last, there is the shawl collar which is still another type of collar construction.

Before beginning to apply a collar, be sure that you understand the meaning of the terms: *fall, break, stand* (see Chapter 2, under *collar*.

Preparing and Attaching an Undercollar—Felled to the Neckline

(*For man's sport coat, blazer, or man-tailored woman's suit*)

METHOD I

I. **Cut the undercollar** (if it was not cut from the pattern when the garment was cut).

A. Use melton or flannel which does not fray. Sometimes self-material is used if it is a firmly woven fabric.
B. Cut the material with the center back on a bias so that the right and left halves will have an identical grainline.
C. Usually there is a ½-in. seam allowance, but if you are not sure of the fit and design, you may provide an extra seam allowance on all outside edges for fitting adjustments.
D. Mark the seamlines.

II. **Cut the collar canvas (interfacing).**

A. For a man's garment this is usually a linen canvas with permanent sizing. Otherwise, it may be cut of hymo. For soft dressmaker collars, wigan or a firm muslin may be desirable. Be sure that the *interfacing is preshrunk* and pressed.
B. Provide extra seam allowance if one was added on the undercollar.
C. Mark the seam allowances.

III. **Stitch the undercollar seam.**

A. Stitch the seam. Press open on wool.
B. Trim the seam to ¼ in.

IV. **Stitch the collar interfacing seam.**

A. Overlap the raw edges at the center back with the seamlines together.
B. Zigzag by machine or catch-stitch by hand.
C. Press flat on wool. Trim off the excess canvas to ⅛ in.

V. Check the creaseline markings.

A. This marking was indicated during the first fitting.

B. At the center back check to see that the fall is deeper than the stand. The fall is a minimum of ⅜ in. wider than the stand (Fig. 190).

C. Check the creaseline markings. The front end of the breakline may be located by matching it to the breakline in the lapel (Fig. 190).

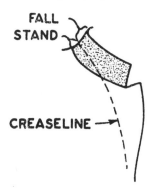

Fig. 190. Checking the creaseline marking.

VI. Baste together the canvas interfacing and the undercollar.

A. Join the canvas and the undercollar by placing the undercollar on top of the canvas, with the wrong side of the wool against the canvas.

B. Baste on the breakline, joining the two together, by placing it flat on the table.

VII. Pad-stitch the stand.

A. Hold the canvas toward you and pad-stitch the stand in vertical rows ¼ in. apart. Begin at the center back and work toward the outside in both halves (Fig. 191).

B. Keep all pad stitches within the seamlines.

VIII. Pad-stitch the fall.

A. Work from the canvas side, holding the collar curved over the left hand.

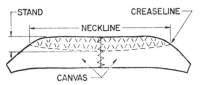

Fig. 191. Pad-stitching the stand.

Fold the stand under at the creaseline.

B. Pad-stitch the fall in horizontal rows, keeping them parallel to the breakline.

C. Pad-stitch only to the marked seam allowances.

D. Roll and shape the corners over your fingers, pulling toward you with the thumb and pushing away from you with the index finger from underneath (Fig. 192).

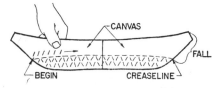

Fig. 192. Pad-stitching the fall.

IX. Shape the undercollar.

A. Lay the collar flat on a cheese block with the canvas side up.

B. Sponge the entire canvas side of the collar.

C. Press the fall and the stand up to the creaseline. Fold the creaseline and press with the fall side down.

D. Press the stand semicircularly, stretching the outer edge especially in the parts that fall directly over the shoulders (A–B)–(A–B), Figure 193. Keep the creaseline in a fold with the stand side up.

E. Press the fall, stretching the outer edges especially in the areas that are directly over the shoulder (C–D)–(C–D), Figure 193. Keep the creaseline in a fold.

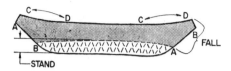

Fig. 193. Shaping the undercollar.

F. Press the creaseline stand side up, to within 2 in. from the end. Press until dry. This should shrink the creaseline some so it fits snugly against the neck.

G. Let the collar dry as shaped. You may dry it over a rolled Turkish towel, a small tailor's ham, or a rounded edge of a cheese block.

X. Retest for fit and design.

A. Pin the undercollar to the neckline and try on.

B. Chalk-mark the neckline seam on the garment.

C. Have the center back of the fall coincide with the center back of the suit.

D. If the neckline seams are more than ½ to ¾ in. longer than before shaping, the collar may need to be recut.

XI. Fell the undercollar to the garment.

A. Cut away the seam allowances on the *neckline* and *gorgeline* of the undercollar.

B. Be sure to leave the seam allowance on the neckline and the gorgeline of the garment.

C. Trim the seam allowance plus ⅟₁₆ in. from the canvas so that the raw edges will not extend outside of the wool; or

D. Some tailors stitch the edge of the stand and the gorgeline on the ma-

chine about ⅛ in. from the edge. This stitching falls inside the **seamline** as the seam allowances are trimmed. It is then felled to the coat.

E. Beginning at the center back, lap the stand edge of the undercollar to the marked seamline of the neck edge, from the lapel notch to lapel notch. Pin and baste. Use **waxed** hand-sewing silk (Fig. 194).

Fig. 194. Felling the under-collar to the garment.

F. Fell, working from the lapel-collar notch on the right front side of the suit to the left.

G. Fell with stitches close together; or

H. Machine-stitch about ⅟₁₆ in. from the raw edge of the wool to fasten it to the coat. (This is not as desirable as hand felling).

XII. Recheck the shape of the ends of the collar.

A. Check the shape of the collar ends in relation to the collar lapel, using the original pattern.

B. Check to see that the two edges of the notch are equal in length.

XIII. Recheck the shape of the fall edge.

Check to see that the fall comes ⅜ in. below the neckline seam at the back and at the shoulder.

XIV. Press the undercollar and the lapel.

A. Hard-press the lapel and the fall of the undercollar.

B. *Do not* press the breakline of the lapel.

XV. Finish the collar-coat seam on the inside of the garment.

A. On the inside of the coat trim the garment and the coat back reinforcement seams, leaving the latter seam longer.

B. Clip where necessary so that the seam will lie flat.

C. Catch-stitch the reinforcement to the canvas stand of the undercollar (Fig. 195).

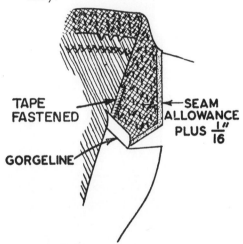

Fig. 195. Finishing the collar.

D. The *loose end of tape* from the lapel breakline may be brought up onto the collar breakline, pulled snugly, and attached by hand along the straight part of the breakline (Fig. 195).

Stitching an Undercollar of Self-Material to the Neckline

(*Used for woman's hard-tailored coat or suit*)

METHOD II

I. Cut the undercollar.

A. Use a self-material of the garment cloth.

B.–D. Same as Method I, step I, B–D.

II.–X. Same as Method I.

XI. Stitch the undercollar of the wool to the suit.

A. *Do not* trim off the seam allowances of the wool.

B. Trim off the seam allowances of the canvas all around the undercollar.

C. Place the neckline of the undercollar on the neckline of the suit, wool sides together.

D. Stitch on the seam allowance from lapel notch to lapel notch.

E. Press the seam open from the notch to the shoulder seam. Press the seam up across the back of the neck between the shoulder seams. Clip and trim seams where necessary.

XII.–XIII. Same as Method I.

XIV. Press the undercollar and the lapel.

The upper collar may be applied to an undercollar of self-material either by hand felling or by machine. *If the hand method is used, the undercollar must have the seam edges finished.* For the machine method, see Chapter 23, p. 98.

XV. Fasten the seam allowance of the undercollar.

A. Trim the seam allowance of the wool undercollar to ¼ to ⅜ in. Some tailors stitch by machine around the stand and fall ¼ to ⅜ in. from edge for added firmness.

B. Turn the trimmed seam allowance over the interfacing smoothly, removing the excess bulk at the corners.

C. Catch-stitch the turned-over seam to the interfacing.

XVI. Press.

CHAPTER 23

Attaching an Upper Collar

(Melton or Self-Material)

THE upper collar, too, may be attached by hand-felling or by machine-stitching. When melton is used, the upper collar is almost always attached by hand-stitching; but with self-material it may be applied in various ways.

Method I. Attaching the Upper Collar to an Undercollar of Melton

(Nonfraying Material)

I. Cut the upper collar (omit if it was cut from the pattern).
A. Cut the upper collar with the center back on the warpwise grain.
B. The cloth collar should be at least 2 in. longer and 1 in. wider than the undercollar cloth.
C. Swing the fall edge about ¼ in. from fold (see Chapter 9, p. 42).

II. Mark the upper collar.
A. Mark the center back with a basting line.
B. Baste the creaseline marking, using the undercollar as a guide.
C. Chalk-mark or baste the seamlines.

III. Shape the upper collar.
Shape the upper collar in the same manner as an undercollar (see Chapter 22, step IX, A–G, pp. 93–94).

IV. Attach the upper collar to the undercollar (baste only).
A. Place the upper collar on top of the undercollar, matching the creaseline and the center back with the wrong sides together.
B. Tailor-baste parallel to and near the creaseline on both the fall and the stand side, slightly easing the material between the two bastings.
C. Some tailors prefer to baste right along the creaseline.
D. Baste ¾ to 1 in. from the outer edge, rolling the collar. Begin at the center back and work toward each end, fulling the upper collar at the corners so the finished collar will be flat (Fig. 197).

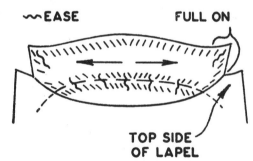

Fig. 197. Basting the upper collar to the undercollar.

E. Trim the seam allowance of the upper collar about ⅜ to ½ in. beyond the edge of the melton undercollar.
F. Turn under the edge of the top collar so it is between the melton undercollar with its attached reinforcement.
G. The folded edge of the upper collar should extend slightly beyond the edge of the undercollar about ⅛ in.

H. At the corners, cut several slashes to miter the corners. Watch the grainline at the collar ends.

I. Baste.

V. Complete the gorgeline.

A. Turn under the seam allowance of the facing on the gorgeline (Fig. 198, A–B).

B. Clip and trim the seam as necessary.

C. Baste and fell in position.

D. Turn under the seam edge on the gorgeline of the upper collar. Clip and trim the seam as needed (Fig. 198).

E. *Do not* remove the ease of the upper collar.

F. Slip-stitch (Fig. 198, A–B) with fine,

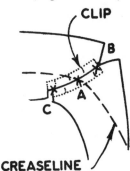

Fig. 198. Completing the gorgeline.

firm stitches, joining the gorgeline of the collar and the facing together.

G. Use thread matching the wool. Be sure the stitches are buried in the wool.

VI. Complete the facing neckline and the upper-collar seam.

A. Since the neckline seam is a continuation of the gorgeline, continue as for the gorgeline (Fig. 198, B–C). Clip and trim as necessary.

B. The seam edges of the two should lie flat and open.

VII. Complete the neckline of the upper collar across the back.

A. Without a facing.

1. The upper collar may extend into the coat when it is lined.

2. Clip the seam edge approximately ½ in. forward of the shoulder end of the front facing (under the facing).

3. Turn down the seam allowance of the upper collar across the back (between clip marks).

4. Catch-stitch the raw edge of the upper collar to the coat back reinforcement. *Be careful not to go through the wool.*

NOTE: On a man's sport coat the seam allowance of the upper collar across the back may be turned under. The lining is placed between the upper collar and the undercollar, and the upper collar is felled into position along the seamline between the facings.

B. With a facing.

1. The facing is fitted to the coat neckline across the back. It is the same width as the end of the front facing at the shoulder.

2. Join the front and back facing at the shoulder with a plain seam. Press open; or

3. The two edges may be turned under so they just meet and slip-stitched together.

4. Across the back of neck, make a plain seam joining the top of the back facing to the upper-collar edge. Press open. You may loosely tack the seams together underneath.

5. The collar-facing seam may be opened or pushed up and graded.

VIII. Finish the outer edge of the upper collar.

A. Fell, using a waxed hand-sewing silk, joining the undercollar and the upper collar around the edge.

B. Begin on the right-hand side of the coat at the lapel-collar notch, with the bulk of the coat toward you.

C. With the collar in your left hand, point the needle straight toward the stand with taut felling stitches. The stitches pass over the raw cut edge of the melton and into the cloth of the upper collar.

Method II. Attaching an Upper Collar to an Undercollar of Self-Material

(Fraying Material)

HAND METHOD

I.–III. Same as Method I.

IV. Attach the upper collar to the undercollar.

A. Baste as in Method I, step IV, A–D. The edges of upper collar should extend ⅛ in. beyond the edges of the undercollar.

B. Turn under the seam allowance around the three sides of the upper collar; baste and catch-stitch raw edges. Trim out the bulk at the corners of the curves.

C. Press.

D. Fell in position as in Method I, step VIII, A–C.

V.–VII. Same as Method I.

MACHINE METHOD

I.–III. Same as in Method I.

IV. Attach the upper collar to the undercollar.

A. Lay the undercollar on the upper collar with the right sides together.

B. Diagonal-baste along the creaseline or a line on each side of the crease-line.

C. Baste around the edges, rolling over the fingers, fulling in slightly at the corners. This allows the collar to lie flat when finished. Check the shape (Fig. 199).

D. Machine-stitch on the seam allowance. Edge-press.

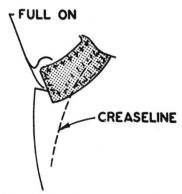

Fig. 199. Checking the shape.

E. Trim the seams by staggering the edges. The top collar may be trimmed to ⅜ to ¼ in. and the under-collar to ¼ to ⅛ in. (+). Trim excess cloth from corners (Fig. 200).

Fig. 200. Trimming the corner.

F. *Optional:* Catch-stitch the seam allowance of the undercollar to the interfacing and the upper-collar seam to the fabric lightly to keep the edges from rolling.

G. Turn the collar right side out and baste with small stitches; three basting stitches, then a backstitch. Keep the seamline rolled slightly under.

V. Complete the gorgeline.
See Method I, step V, A–G, and step VI, A–B.

VI. Press.
Hard-press, then off-press.

VII. Complete the neckline and the upper collar.
See Method I, step VII, A–B.

VIII. Press.

CHAPTER **24**

Other Collar Methods

Preparing the Collar Before Attaching

IN A softly tailored garment it may be desirable to prepare the collar before attaching it to the garment.

I. Make and shape the undercollar.
See Chapter 22, steps I–X, pp. 92–94. Use self-material.

II. Make and shape the upper collar.
See Chapter 23, Method I, steps I–III, p. 96, and steps I–IV, p. 98. (Hand method or machine method.)

III. Press.
Hard-press, then off-press.

IV. Attach the completed collar to the garment.
A. See Chapter 22, Method I, step XI, p. 94; or
B. Method II, step XI, p. 95.
C. See Chapter 23, Method I, steps V, VI, VII, p. 97.

Attaching a Shawl Collar

Fashion dictates the use of a shawl collar on many ladies' suits. The under-collar and forepart of the shawl collar are cut in one piece. There is a seam found in both the upper and under collars.

I. Mark the seamlines of the collar.
A. Mark the seamline of the shoulders, neck, and shawl-collar extensions.

B. Mark the diagonal clip line at the corner where shoulders and the collar extension meet.

II. Stay-stitch the raw edges.
A. Stitch around the clip mark, as in Figure 203. Turn exactly at the point. Do this for both corners.

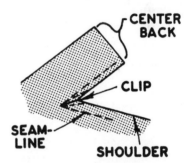

Fig. 203. Stay-stitching the raw edges.

B. A firm lightweight material may be placed under the area before stay-stitching, giving added body for less firm material.

III. Sew the center back seams.
Sew the center seam of the garment back, if any. Sew the center-back seam of the collar extensions. Press these seams open.

IV. Put the shoulder seams together.
A. Match the notches. Pin them together all the way up to the point at the end of the slip mark.
B. Baste and stitch to that point.
C. Do this for both shoulders (Fig. 204).

99

V. Mark the point of the clip mark.

A. Stick a pin across the point at the end of the clip mark.

B. Put it through the stitching at the point. Be exact (Fig. 204).

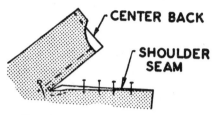

Fig. 204.   Marking the points of the clip mark.

VI. Cut along the clip mark.

A. Be careful not to cut the back seam allowance when slipping in the shears.

B. Cut as far as you can; the pin will stop the shears.

C. Clip both corners.

VII. Clip around the neckline at the back.

Clip down from the edges almost to the seamline to ease the curve (Fig. 205).

VIII. Pin the collar extension to the back of the neck.

A. Match the centers and the notches.

B. Spread open the clipped corners until the collar extension turns each corner neatly.

C. Pin and baste (Figure 205).

IX. Stitch the back of the neck seam.

A. Since the edges have been stay-stitched, start at the shoulder edge (Fig. 205, A); stitch past the first corner (Fig. 205, B), the machine needle sinking into the point.

B. Continue stitching on around the back to the neck, past the second corner (Fig. 205, C) and out to the end of the seam allowance (Fig. 205, D).

C. Press the seams open.

X. Put the front facings and the back of the neck facing together the same way.

XI. Baste the shaped interfacing to the inside of the two coat fronts.

A. Overlap the center back seam of the collar and catchstitch.

B. Baste across the back of the neck and shoulder seams.

C. Try on the garment and check again for the breakline and the stand of the collar. Mark and baste this line (Fig. 206, A–B).

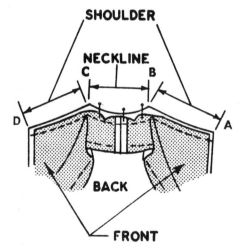

Fig. 205.   Joining the collar extension to the neck.

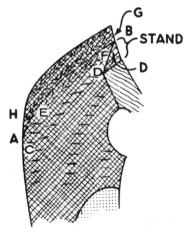

Fig. 206.   Basting the interfacing.

D. Tailor-baste on the garment side of the breakline about an inch from the line (Fig. 206, C–D).

E. Baste the interfacing to the coat below the breakline (see Chapter 16, p. 76). Keep the basting 1½ in. from the seam edges.

XII. Pad-stitch the stand of the under-collar.

Pad-stitch the stand of the collar (see Chapter 22, Method I, step VII, p. 93).

XIII. Pad-stitch below the breakline.

Make a row or two of pad-stitching (Fig. 206, E–F) just below the breakline.

XIV. Pad-stitch the collar.

Pad-stitch the left side of the collar, beginning at G in Figure 206 at the center back down to H and then back to the center back without turning the garment. Roll over fingers to shape. Continue the pad-stitching until half of the collar is completed, leaving the seam edge free. On the right side of the collar begin at H and pad-stitch to G without turning the garment.

XV. Trim the interfacing.

See Chapter 18, p. 80.

XVI. Tape the front edges.

A. Trim the canvas the seam allowance plus ⅛ in.

B. Attach the tape (see Chapter 18, p. 80) from the bottom to the top button on up the breakline; continue down on the other side. Do not tape the outer edge of the collar (Fig. 207). You may tape from C–D in Figure 207 but not beyond the shoulders.

XVII. Attach the facing (includes the upper collar).

A. See Chapter 21, p. 89, for the techniques of applying the front facing.

B. With the right sides together, pin, baste, and stitch the seam at the center back. Press.

C. Baste the facing to the garment on the creaseline. Then ease the collar into position as in the directions for the lapel in Chapter 21, p. 89.

D. Stitch, turn, trim the seams, and finish as explained in Chapter 21, p. 90.

E. Attach the facing loosely to the canvas part way up from the bottom.

F. When fastening the collar at the neck and shoulder edge, allow for roll in the top collar. Use a back-stitch on the seamline for this operation, without turning-under the top collar.

XVIII. Press.

A. Hard-press the facing edges. Off-press.

B. Do not put a crease in the breakline.

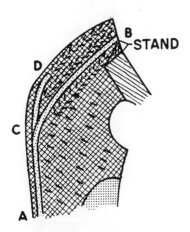

Fig. 207. Taping the front edges

CHAPTER 25

Constructing and Setting in Sleeves

(Finishing the Bottom of Sleeves and Fastening Shoulder Pads)

TAILORS prepare the armhole in different ways for the setting-in of the sleeves. Some stay-stitch the armhole by machine; others baste-tape around the armscye; still others use a drawing-in stitch merely to stay the edge over the upper half of the sleeve and draw-in the lower-half ⅜ in. in the front and ¼ in. in the back. It is generally agreed that if tape is used, only the lower half or back of the armscye should be taped. This tape should be shaped and clipped at the free edge. Two exceptions are children's clothes and stretching cloth, which may be taped around the entire armscye. In most dressmaker suits, the interfacing extends into the armhole and no tape is used.

Regardless of the method used for staying, the armscye ought to be checked for size once again before the sleeves are set in. In a man's coat, the armscye generally measures about one half the coat size. Both armscyes should be the same size. If one shoulder is lower and the shoulder seam has been taken in, the armscye would have to be recut to compensate. The standard sleeve is 2¼ to 2¾ in. larger than the armscye, but this varies with the style and fashion trends. For gabardines, which do not shrink well, it would be desirable to have a smaller sleeve. Lightweight canvas may be stitched into the sleeve seams. (See p. 104, Step VIII.)

I. Mark the sleeves.

A. Thread-mark the hemline.
B. Tailor-tack where the sleeve is to match the shoulder seam and the underarm seams. (This may have been done following the first fitting.)
C. Baste the line of the warp and filling threads in the top of the sleeve (Fig. 210).

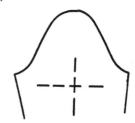

Fig. 210. Marking the sleeve.

II. Make the front sleeve seam.

A. Baste the front seam of the upper sleeve onto the lower sleeve seam.
B. Stitch the seam and press it open.

III. Shape the sleeve.

A. Lay the sleeve seam over the center of the cheese block or the ironing board.
B. Sponge the undersleeve (A, Fig. 211).
C. Stretch the back edge (for the elbow) of the front seam slightly, about ½ in. (Fig. 211, A).
D. Sponge at B in Figure 211.
E. Shrink out by holding in the fullness

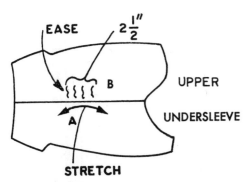

Fig. 211. Shaping the sleeve.

with the left hand in a 2½-in. area
(Fig. 211).

F. In a one-piece sleeve, shrink in front
for the bend of the arm and stretch
slightly for the elbow to give shape.

IV. Make the back sleeve seam.

A. Fold the sleeve and let it fall natu-
rally to aid in determining the position of the back seam.

B. Baste the back seam of the upper
and lower sleeve. Ease the fullness of
the upper sleeve between the notches.

C. Stitch. Sponge and press the seam
open, wrong side out, on a sleeve
board.

D. Avoid pressing wrinkles in the elbow
area where shaping was done.

V. Shape the cap of the sleeve.

A. The sleeves are fuller by 2¼ in. (1½
in. on the upper sleeves and ¾ in. on
the undersleeve) than the armscye.

B. Run three rows of fine running
stitches with the center one on the
seamline and the other two ⅛ in. to
each side of the center one; or

C. Run two rows of medium-length machine stitch with the tension loos-
ened *slightly.* Place one row on the
seamline, and the other row ⅛ in.
outside of the stitching line toward
the raw edge. This method is preferred by some because there is no
danger of press marks on the upper
part of sleeve.

D. Draw up the gathering threads in
the upper sleeve 1½ in., and in the
undersleeve ¾ in.

E. Place the sleeve over a small tailor's
ham, a press mitt, or the end of a
sleeve board. Sponge just the seam
allowance. Shrink in the fullness.
Avoid wrinkles. *Avoid pressing down
into the sleeve* (Fig. 212).

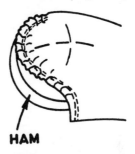

Fig. 212. Shaping the
cap of the sleeve.

F. After the cap is shaped, allow it to
dry over a soft pad or shoulder pad
until thoroughly dry.

VI. Set the sleeve into the coat.

A. Pin the left sleeve into the coat beginning at the front notch. Pin the
back notch at the back seam. Pin in
the sleeve over the cap.

B. Baste, beginning at the front notch
over the top of the sleeve, toward
the bottom, around to the front
notch. Be careful to retain the shape
of the cap at the top of the sleeve.

C. Begin the right sleeve at the back
notch. Then stitch over the top of
the cap.

D. Reinforcement may be basted (tape)
onto the sleeve seam from the coat
side, centering the tape over the
seam. Pull slightly taut. Some tailors
begin at the shoulder, extending the
tape around the back almost to the
front notch. Check the fit of the
sleeve to see that the vertical grainline is perpendicular to the floor
(Fig. 213, a). If the grainline points

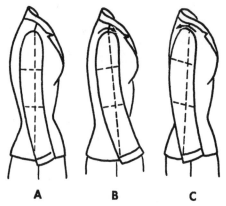

| A | B | C |

Fig. 213. Checking the fit of the sleeve.

forward, remove the sleeve and shift as indicated in Figure 213, b. If the grainline points toward the back, remove the sleeve and shift as indicated in Figure 213, c.

E. Stitch the seam, holding the sleeve topmost. Control the distribution of ease and stitch *straight* with a fairly small stitch.

F. Remove the bastings.

VII. Press the armscye line.

A. Hard-tailored effect (blazers, men's coats).
   1. Clip the seam allowance at the notches.
   2. Press the seam edges open at the top half of the armscye line. You may trim to ½ in.
   3. Clip the coat-side seam edges. You may have to shrink in the sleeve-side seam edges more.
   4. The seam edges underarm will turn upward toward the arm. Clip and trim the seams to ⅜ in.

B. Softly tailored effect (most women's suits and coats).
   1. Do not press. (You may finger press.)
   2. Push the seam edges at the top of the sleeve into the sleeve.
   3. Grade the edges, leaving the sleeve seam ½ in. Trim the other seam

edges to ⅜ in. You may cut triangles out of the upper half of the sleeve to remove excess bulk.
   4. The underarm seams will turn upward. Trim the seams to ⅜ in. and clip to ⅛ in. of the seamline stitching.

VIII. Fasten the canvas to the sleeve seam (lightweight reinforcements may be stitched into sleeve seams).

A. From the right side of the garment run a basting around the armscye, just inside of the seam.

B. Go through all the layers.

C. Turn the coat to the wrong side and loosely permanent-baste the reinforcement to the edge of the seam.

D. Remove the first basting.

E. Trim the excess canvas and padding around the armscye. The raw edges of the reinforcement should extend ¼ in. beyond the stitching line on the upper half of the sleeve. At the lower half, trim close.

IX. Pad the crown of the sleeve.

A. Use cotton felt or sheet wadding. Gauze or cheesecloth may be substituted. Sleeve-head wadding may be purchased for this purpose, also.

B. For a coat or a man's garment, cut two strips 4 in. (the length between notches over the top of the sleeve + 2 in.). For a lightweight garment a 2-in. strip may be wide enough.

C. Fold the strip lengthwise until it is about 1 in. wide. Stitch lengthwise in the middle with a fairly long machine stitch.

D. Loosely permanent-baste one strip in the upper half of each sleeve. Place the strip between the extending sleeve seam pad-canvas and the sleeve itself, beginning at the front notch and extending somewhat past the back notch. Place the folded edge of the sleeve head even with the raw edge of the sleeve seam. When using a purchased sleeve head, place the smooth edge of the sleeve head toward the sleeve. This gives the top of the sleeve a smooth soft-rolled look.

As noted on "General Procedure Sheets," often the hem of the sleeve is finished and the lining is inserted in the sleeve before the sleeve is attached to the armscye.

Vent (Completing the Bottom Before Setting in the Sleeve)

I. Stitch the front sleeve and press open. See step II on p. 102.

II. Cut the reinforcement.
A. Cut the reinforcement of hymo, wigan, or muslin. Wigan or muslin is preferred for lighter weight wools.
B. Cut on the bias and about ¾ in. wider than the length of the vent. For a man's sport coat the reinforcement is usually 3 in. wide.
C. On the underlap edge, cut the shape of the sleeve, and on the overlap side cut straight just beyond the seamline (Fig. 214).

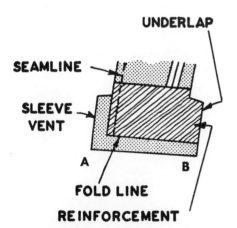

Fig. 214. Making the cuff.

D. Trim the wigan the seam allowance width on the upper sleeve edge at A in Figure 214. Trim the wigan ¼ in. on the vent edge, B.

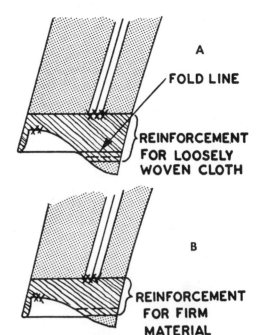

Fig. 215. Attaching the reinforcement.

III. Attach the reinforcement.
A. On loosely woven materials, extend the reinforcement ¼ in. beyond the foldline (Fig. 215, a). In firm materials, bring the reinforcement just short of the foldline at the bottom (Fig. 215, b).
B. Tailor-baste first from the wool side.
C. Turn to the inside and permanent-baste or catch-stitch the reinforcement into position. Use matching thread to baste or catch-stitch lightly above the foldline if it does not extend over the fold; otherwise, tack lightly on each side of the folding or in the foldline. Also fasten along

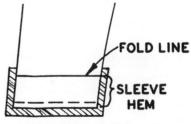

Fig. 216A. Stitching the reinforcement.

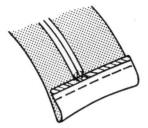

Fig. 216B.   Folding back
the sleeve.

the seamline of sides. The top may
be tacked at the seamlines or catch-
stitched. Be sure that these stitches
do not show on the right side of the
garment.

D. For a man's sport coat and other
garments a machine method is used.
Place the reinforcement against the
wrong side of the sleeve extending
½ in. beyond the bottom of the
sleeve to the foldline. Stitch ¼ in.
from the sleeve bottom (Fig. 216, a).
Turn back the sleeve on the foldline
and attach at the seam (Fig. 216, b).

IV. **Prepare the bound buttonholes.**
See Chapter 19, p. 82.

V. **Complete the hems and the vent.**

A. Check with the pattern for directions for finishing the vent.

B. In a two-piece sleeve, the upper part
of the sleeve overlaps the underpart.

C. On an overlap, fold back the vent
and hem and form a diagonal seam
from A to B (Fig. 217) forming a
mitered corner. Stitch a seam from

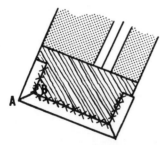

Fig. 217.   Forming a
mitered corner.

the wrong side; trim. On the underlap turn back about ¼ in. and catch-
stitch the raw edge to the reinforcement. Miter at the bottom onto the
reinforcement; catch-stitch into position; or

D. Turn back and baste both sides and
then turn up the bottoms, felling the
turned up edges. The hem may be
attached loosely to the reinforcement
or at the seams (Fig. 218). This

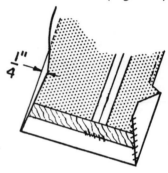

Fig. 218.   Basting the hem
and reinforcement.

method is preferred for sport coats.

E. Hard-press, then off-press.

VI. **Finish the buttonholes.**

A. Finish the facing side of the bound
buttonholes; or

B. Work false-worked buttonholes if
they are to be used.

VII. **Complete the elbow seams.**

A. Clip the sleeve seam diagonally at
the upper end of the vent opening.

**CATCH STITCH
EDGES**

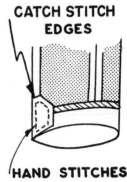

HAND STITCHES
Fig. 219.   Attaching the vents.

B. Baste, stitch, and press the seam open.

VIII. **Attach the vents to position.**

A. Place the vents in position.
B. On the wrong side, catch-stitch together the raw edges of the clipped seams at the top of the vent (Fig. 219); or
C. On the wrong side, attach the underlap by hand. Be sure that the stitches do not show on the right side (Fig. 219); or
D. Catch-stitch on the wrong side at the top of the vent the width of the hem. You may make a French tack to hold the vent closed (Fig. 220).

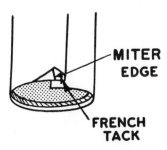

MITER EDGE

FRENCH TACK

Fig. 220. French tack to close the vent.

E. Buttons are often used on the vents for decoration (Chapter 32, p. 128).

Hem

I. **Complete the sleeve seams.**

Complete the hem before or after the sleeve is set into the garment.

II. **Cut the reinforcement.**

A. Cut the reinforcement of wigan, muslin, or hymo.
B. Cut on the bias and about ¾ in. wider than hem.

III. **Attach the reinforcement.**

Place the reinforcement in position

(see step III, A–D, p. 105 under "Vent").

IV. **Complete the hem.**

A. Turn back the wool hem over the reinforcement.
B. Baste and press lightly.
C. Catch-stitch the raw edge of the wool hem lightly to the reinforcement.

Fastening the Shoulder Pads

I. **Place the shoulder pads in position.**

A. Try on the garment and adjust it to the proper position.
B. A shaped pad should rest firmly on the shoulders with usually ¼ in. extending beyond the seamline. This may vary with fashion trends (Fig. 221).

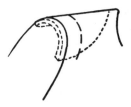

Fig. 221. Fastening a shoulder pad.

C. The pad rests on the shoulder and goes under the front of the facing.
D. Pin the pads securely from the right side of the garment.
E. Placing a hand under the shoulder, baste on the right side from notch to notch, approximately 1 in. from the seam (Fig. 221).

II. **Sew the pads into position.**

A. Using a stab stitch, attach the pad in the shoulder seam.
B. Attach it loosely, but firmly, to the armscye seam at each side where it falls along the seamline.
C. Tack it loosely in two or three other places.

CHAPTER 26

Hemming the Garment

THERE are three common construction methods used in hemming the tailored garment, namely, (1) constructing the hem of the garment with a curve at the lower front edge; (2) constructing the hem of the garment with the corner at the lower front edge; and (3) constructing the hem of a coat across the facing. These three methods will be discussed below.

Hems of lined suits do not have to be finished with a seam binding ribbon. Coat hems of nonfraying material are pinked; otherwise they are edged with seam ribbon or bias. Jacket hems and sleeve hems are generally 1¼ to 1½ in. deep, and the average coat hem is 2 to 2½ in. deep.

Method I. Constructing the Hem of the Garment With a Curve at the Lower Front Edge

I. Mark the hemline and baste.

A. The hemline should be hung while the garment is being fitted.

B. Mark the hemline by basting.

C. Turn the hem up and baste into position close to the fold. Try on to check the length.

D. Trim so the hem is even in width.

II. Cut the reinforcement. Omit the step for a man's sport coat.

A. Cut a bias of wigan ½ to ¾ in. wider than the hem and the length of the hem plus the seam allowance, if it has to be pieced, plus 1 in.

B. Muslin may be substituted or a lightweight hymo on a heavy coating.

C. If the suit coat is lined from the waist to the hem, use that reinforcement for the hem rather than an added bias strip.

III. Attach the reinforcement.

A. On a less firm fabric extend the bias ⅛ to ¼ in. below the marked hemline, but on firm fabrics bring it just to the hemline (Fig. 224).

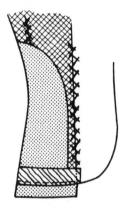

Fig. 224. Attaching the reinforcement.

B. Directions for attaching the reinforcement may be found in Chapter 25, step III, C, p. 105.

C. Extend the strip ½ in. under the front facing on each side (Fig. 224).

D. For a machine method of applying wigan (see Chapter 25, step III, D, p. 106).

IV. Shrink out the excess fullness.

A. Run a fine gathering thread along the top of the hem.

B. Pull the thread fairly snug, distributing the fullness evenly.

C. Place brown paper between the reinforcement and the hem, and press the hem against the brown paper and the reinforcement on a cheese block. Shrink out the fullness (see Chapter 8, p. 39) (Fig. 225).

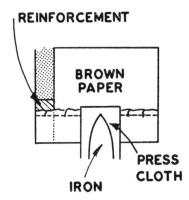

Fig. 225. Shrinking out the fullness.

D. Be careful at the seams so as not to bring the hemline to a slight point.
E. Dry. Remove the basting.

V. **Fasten the raw edge of the front facing to the hem.**

A. Catch-stitch finely or fell the raw edge of the front facing to the hem (Fig. 226).

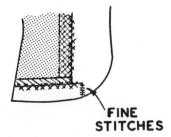

Fig. 226. Fastening the raw edge to the facing of the hem.

B. Use matching silk thread.
C. On material which ravels, the facing may be turned under slightly.

VI. **Attach the hem and the reinforcement.**

A. Catch-stitch (or running catch-stitch) the hem to the bias reinforcement (Fig. 226).
B. Attach the reinforcement securely at the seams and loosely to the wool.

Method II. Constructing the Hem of a Garment With a Corner at the Lower Front Edge

I.–IV. Same as in Method I.

V. Mark the hemline of the facing.
   Mark the hemline of the facing so that it is slightly shorter than the coat hem — $\frac{1}{16}$ to $\frac{1}{8}$ in.

VI. Trim away the excess cloth of the hem and the facing.

A. Lay the facing open.
B. Allow $\frac{3}{8}$ to $\frac{1}{2}$-in. seam allowance along the lower foldlines of the hem and the facing (Fig. 227).
C. Allow 1 to 1½ in. of the hem to extend under the facing (Fig. 227).

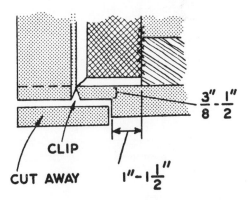

Fig. 227. Trimming the excess.

VII. Fasten the raw edge of the front facing to the hem.

A. See Method I, step V, above.
B. At the lower foldline of the hem and

facing, slip-stitch or fell the facing to the coat hem on a ⅟₁₆–⅛ in. diagonal so that the facing will not show (Fig. 228).

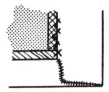

Fig. 228. Attaching the hem and facing.

VIII. **Attach the hem and the reinforcement.**

A. See Method I, step VI, above.

Constructing the Hem of a Coat Across the Facing

Usually the hems of a coat and the lining are finished separately. On material which frays, the hems are finished with tape but on nonfraying material they are often pinked and attached with no binding.

I.–IV. Same as Method I (pp. 108–109).

V. **Attach the hem and reinforcement to the coat.**

A. Hem across the facing.
B. Nonfraying material.
   1. Pink the raw edge of the hem.
   2. Turn back the top edge of the coat hem about ¼ in. and catch the coat and then the reinforcement continuing along the hem. The reinforcement may or may not extend above the hem. If the

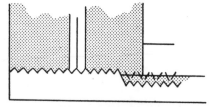

Fig. 229A. Attaching the hem and reinforcement to the coat.

reinforcement extends above the hem, the hemline will be less conspicuous. Use a running catch-stitch (Fig. 229A).

C. Fraying material.
   1. Backstitch or machine-stitch the seam binding ribbon to the top edge of the coat hem, easing on the seam binding.
   2. Trim the bias reinforcement so that it does not show above the tape and catch. Turn down the tape, and attach the hem loosely to the garment with a running catch-stitch (Fig. 229B). The stitches will fall between the wrong side of the hem and the reinforcement (Fig. 229C).

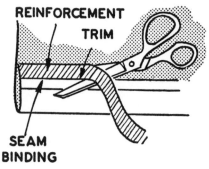

Fig. 229B. Trimming the bias reinforcement.

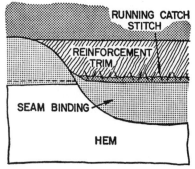

Fig. 229C. A running catch stitch.

VI. **Fasten the raw edge of the front facing to the hem.**

A. See Method I, step V, A–C (p. 109), or:

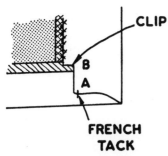

CLIP

B
A

FRENCH
TACK

Fig. 230. French tack to
hold the facing in position.

B. Turn under the raw edge of the facing and the hem edge between A
and B, clipping the facing at B (Fig.
230). Slip-stitch the two edges together, free from the coat hem.
C. A French tack may be used to hold
the facing in position (Fig. 230).

D. The lower edge of the facing and
hem is left open (Fig. 230).

If the coat is too bulky when this
method is used, the excess on just the
facing may be trimmed away. Later, if
the garment needs to be lengthened,
then just the facing has to be pieced.

Occasionally, lead weights may be used
at the underarm and back seams to hold
the garment in position. They are usually
enclosed in a square of lining material
and attached to the hem before it is
placed into position.

Chain weights of lacquered brass plated
steel may be used to prevent jackets from
riding up. The upper edge of the chain
is hand sewn to the garment by placing it
under the fold of the lining or at the top
of the hem.

CHAPTER 27

Pressing the Garment Shell Before the Lining Is Attached

AFTER the wool garment is completed and before the lining is attached, the jacket should be pressed well. The process requires much time and patience. In some cases, the sleeve lining may be attached at the sleeve bottom and basted in around the sleeve near the lower armscye.

Most tailors dry press all the edges to set them. The top press cloth is sponged and then is pressed dry, which may result in a shiny surface. The edges may be beaten, also, to flatten them. It is better to allow the garment to dry thoroughly and "set," and then off-press to remove the shine (see Chapter 8, p. 38, for the use of press cloths).

I. Remove the bastings.

A. Remove all the bastings except the one marking the center front.

B. The edges may be pressed slightly first to set them before removing the bastings.

II. Edge-press all around the coat.

A. Use a cheese block, a wood press block, or a slightly padded ironing board.

B. Beginning with the left front at the top button, place the inside of the garment up, and hard-press a little more than the width of the iron. Continue around to the right front top button (Fig. 233, A–B).

III. Press the revers and the collar.

A. Turn the coat over so that the right side of the garment is up.

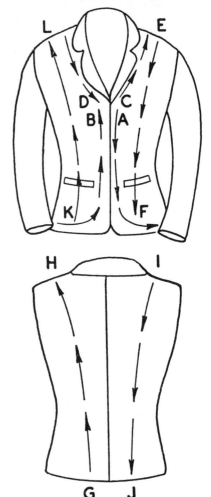

Fig. 233.   Pressing the garment.

B. Begin at the bottom of the left revers and continue around to the bottom of the right revers (Fig. 233, C–D).

C. Press the creaseline of the collar from the inside over a ham.

IV. Press the body of the coat.

A. Press the body of the garment on the right side over a ham cushion, using a damp press cloth. Begin at the left side of the garment. Press lightly. Be careful to retain the shape of the garment (Fig. 233, E–F, G–H).

1. Shoulder.

    a. The shoulder may be pressed by holding a press mitt under the shoulder; or

    b. Press on the end of a sleeve board.

2. Underarm.

    a. Turn the coat to the wrong side.

    b. Place the under armscye uppermost over the end of a sleeve board.

    c. Press the lower half of the armhole, creasing it at the seam toward the body of the garment.

3. Pocket.

    a. Beat the pocket to flatten it if necessary.

    b. If it is a flap pocket, lift and press out the outline of the flap.

4. Lower back and upper back. Be careful to retain the shaped areas over the hip and the shoulder blades (Fig. 233, G–H).

B. Repeat on the right side of the garment, beginning with the upper back and reversing the above procedure (Fig. 233, I–J, K–L).

V. Press the sleeves.

A. Press the sleeves lengthwise over a sleeve board.

B. The sleeve cap is pressed *lightly* over a hand pad. Avoid pressing the seamline.

C. The shoulder seam may be pressed lightly.

D. Crease the sleeve in the seam against the body of coat, by turning the coat inside out, with the end of the sleeve board into the armhole, and the armpit of the coat uppermost.

VI. Press the collar and the revers.

A. Press the collar from the right side over a ham.

B. If the cloth leaves imprints, place brown paper between the collar edge and the garment.

C. Press the creaseline of the collar. This may extend no farther than 1 in. onto the revers.

D. Over a ham, press the surface of the revers, maintaining a soft roll of revers with the facing side up. Hold the roll line of the lapel curved inward when pressing at the point where the creaseline of the revers and the collar meets.

E. Set the roll by pulling gently and hand rolling along the creaseline. Do *not* press a fold along the creaseline of the revers.

CHAPTER 28

Making a Tailored Eyelet or Worked Buttonhole

THE beginner may feel that a tailored eyelet buttonhole is quite difficult to make, but with a little practice the skill can be developed. This type of buttonhole is used primarily on men's sport jackets, fly fronts, and trousers, or on a women's hard-tailored suit coat or coat.

I. Mark the position of the buttonhole.
A. See Chapter 19, step I, A–G, p. 82.
B. Center the eyelet or triangle on the center front line.
C. You may hand-baste with small stitches to mark the buttonhole location, rather than machine-stitch as stated in G above, if desired.

II. Prepare the coat for the buttonhole.
A. See Chapter 19, step II, A–D, p. 83.
B. Some tailors make the buttonhole through the canvas, without removing the hymo.
C. A narrow ⅛-in. rectangle may be machine-stitched around the buttonhole marking to make a stiffer buttonhole.

III. Cut the buttonhole.
A. It is suggested that you cut a practice buttonhole to check the correct

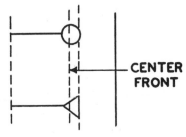

Fig. 236. Cutting the buttonhole.

length and to develop skill in cutting.
B. Cut the length of the buttonhole on the filling (crosswise) thread not quite to eyelet end (Fig. 236).
C. A buttonhole cutter or ⅛-in. punch may be used, if one is available which cuts the marked line and the eyelet at once.
D. Using a buttonhole scissors.
  1. Adjust the scissors for the correct length of the buttonhole.
  2. Cut on the marked line.
  3. For cutting the eyelet, see F below.
E. Using a scissors.
  1. Insert the sharp point at the eyelet end and cut on the marked line.
  2. For cutting the eyelet, see F below.
F. Cutting the eyelet (¹⁄₁₆–³⁄₁₆ in. in diameter, depending on the weight of the material).
  1. Cut out and remove a small triangle with the straight edge parallel to the edge of the coat and centered on the center front line; or
  2. Snip in a circular fashion in short radiating lines. A stiletto will help round out the eyelet.

IV. Reinforce the edges to prevent fraying.
A. Overcast or buttonhole with about eight stitches per inch around the edge with fine silk thread, or machine-stitch around the edge; or
B. Wax the edges. Run a warm knife over beeswax, remove any excess wax

on paper, and then run the knife over the buttonhole edges. Avoid staining the fabric with the wax.

V. Pad the buttonhole with a foundation cord.

A. Use gimp about 3 in. long (heavy cord) or prepare a stranding thread. For a stranding thread use medium weight linen thread or two to four lengths of buttonhole thread twisted. For a double thread, use about a 2-yd. length.

B. To prepare the stranding thread, double the thread, pull it over beeswax, then twist it until it is firm and smooth. Twist by placing the thread in the left hand, and rubbing downward with the right. When a partial length is twisted, wrap it around the left thumb and continue twisting. When using buttonhole twist, you may want to twist another double length with the first double-twisted length. Some tailors thread the cord and knot it, placing a needle end into an ironing board. Then holding the knotted end taut, twist as suggested above. After twisting rub the twisted thread through beeswax, and smooth it with absorbent paper, cloth, or a warm iron.

C. With a knot at the end of the foundation cord, insert it ¼ to ⅜ in. from the bar end of the buttonhole (Fig. 237). Bring the cord up at the bar

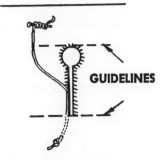

Fig. 237. Padding the buttonhole.

end. Allow the knot to rest on top of the fabric, if the material is closely woven. If the material is loosely woven, the knot can be buried between the two layers of material.

D. Lay the foundation cord along the cut edge bringing it toward the eyelet end. Wind excess cord around a pin inserted near the eyelet end (Fig. 237).

E. Hold the cord firmly with the thumb while working the buttonhole stitch over it.

F. Beginners may find it helpful to overcast the cord lightly in position.

G. If the gimp is used as a foundation cord, lay it along the edge where the buttonhole stitch begins (see Step VII below, Fig. 237) and after seven or eight buttonhole stitches have been made, pull up the gimp to bury the end.

VI. Prepare the twist.

A. Use buttonhole twist in silk usually a shade darker than the cloth.

B. Allow about one yard of twist for an inch of buttonhole.

C. Draw the twist gently over the beeswax, and then between absorbent paper or a cloth and a warm iron.

D. This waxing prevents the twist from gnarling and knotting.

VII. Work a buttonhole stitch.

A. Hold the garment in the left hand, with the eyelet at your left, so that you may work from right to left, beginning at the bar end.

B. Fasten the thread without a knot and bring it out at the bar end.

C. Bring the needle through the opening and at right angles to it, pushing it only halfway through the cloth. The needle comes out below the opening. You may hold your thumbnail close to the stitchline as a guide for the depth of each stitch.

D. Grasp the double thread near the eye

of the needle and cross it (the thread forms a figure eight) passing it under the point of the needle from right to left (Figs. 238 and 239).

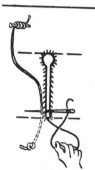

Fig. 238. The buttonhole stitch.

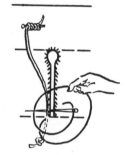

Fig. 239. The button-hole stitch.

E. Pull the needle out and pull it directly upward almost to the end.

F. Then grasp the thread between the thumb and the index finger, pulling the thread toward you, then away, to set the purl.

G. If a stranding thread is used as a foundation cord, after four or five stitches, release the pin and pull the thread so the knot is pulled between the layers of fabric. Then rewind the thread again along the cut edge. Gimp is pulled taut after the buttonhole is completed or when it is half done and again when finished.

H. Continue with the stitches close together.

I. At the eyelet end work for shape.

Release the pin holding the foundation cord. Let the foundation cord lie under the stitches and set the purl high so that more stitches can be placed here for strength.

J. Lay the foundation cord along the other side of the opening and twist the excess around a pin at the bar end.

K. Continue the buttonhole stitch to the bar end, ending exactly opposite the first stitch taken.

L. Draw the needle through the purl of the first stitch, holding the end together firmly.

VIII. Fasten the foundation cord.

A. Draw up the foundation cord firmly. Hold a stiletto at the eyelet to shape it.

B. Fasten it securely on the wrong side of the garment. Gimp may be threaded on a large needle and drawn between layers of cloth. Cut off about 1 in. from the end of the buttonhole.

IX. Work the bar end.

A. Make a bar of three or four stitches (Fig. 240, a).

B. Have each stitch extend from the depth of a stitch of one side to the depth of a stitch on the other side.

C. Work three or four purled stitches over the bar with the purl toward the buttonhole; or

D. Work an over-and-over stitch over the bar like a satin stitch (Fig. 240, b).

E. Fasten the thread on the wrong side.

   A

   B

Fig. 240. Making the bar end.

X. Press and shape the buttonhole.

A. Steam and press the buttonhole, pulling it gently to shape with the thumb and index finger.

B. Use a bodkin or stiletto to shape the eyelet end.

C. Stay-baste the opening shut with diagonal basting.

European tailors often use a different method of working a buttonhole beginning at the opposite end of the buttonhole opening and forming a loop first. The end result is similar.

False Buttonholes

This type of buttonhole is used on sleeves and vents and sometimes on the lapel of a man's sport garment.

I. Mark the buttonhole.

A. See Chapter 19, step I, A–F, p. 82.

B. Mark the location of the buttonhole with a basting thread.

II. Make the buttonhole.

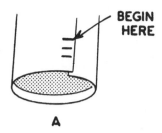

A

B

Fig. 241. Using a chain stitch to make a false buttonhole.

A. Use buttonhole twist and the chain stitch.

B. Begin at the folded edge of the vent and work the chain stitch continuously around the marking (Fig. 241, a and b).

C. Fasten the thread at the end.

D. Attach the button at the broken end near the vent fold.

CHAPTER **29**

Applying the Interlining

INTERLINING is commonly used in winter coats to be worn in a cold climate. The interlining may be of lamb's wool, chamois, wool, or napped cotton flannel. The trend today is toward a sun-backed lining in which the interlining is of wool or a synthetic and woven with the lining. Also metal-insulated linings are popular. A synthetic interlining (urethane foam) may be inserted as a separate interlining or attached to a lining by quilting. Quilted linings are often backed with wool. With the latter types of lining and interlining combinations, the two are inserted as a lining.

Interlinings may be inserted by stitching seams with the corresponding lining seams, which may result in bulk in heavy materials, and pucker at seamline. Also, if the garment lining needs to be replaced, the interlining would also have to be removed. The other method, preferred by the author, is to apply the interlining separately. This perhaps is the most satisfactory method for heavier garments.

1. Cut the interlining.

A. Follow the pattern instructions, if they are included in your pattern; or
B. Use the lining pattern.
C. Cut as the lining pattern, excluding the hem at the bottom of the coat and the sleeve hem. Do not put a pleat in the back of the interlining.
D. Sometimes, only the outer sleeve is interlined.

II. Mark the interlining.
Mark the darts, notches, and seamlines.

III. Construct the interlining.

A. Slash the darts in the center. Lap the raw edges. Machine-stitch or catch-stitch the edges together. Trim to remove bulk (Figs. 244A and B).

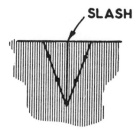

Fig. 244A. Slash the darts in the center.

Fig. 244B. Stitching the edges together.

Fig. 244C. Making the lap seam.

B. Construct the seams.
   1. Lap the shoulder, underarm, and any other seams flat, seamline on seamline, and machine-stitch or catch-stitch (Fig. 244C).
   2. Seams may be trimmed to remove bulk.
   3. If machine-stitching is used, use a longer stitch and looser tension than for normal stitching; or
   4. Pin and baste the interlining into the coat. Then overlap the interlining seams over the coat seams and catch-stitch into position. This method is desirable for fitted garments.
C. If a partial sleeve lining is used, join the sleeve interlining to the outer sleeve lining.

IV. **Attaching the interlining.**

A. Turn the coat wrong side out and place it on a dress form or hang it on a hanger. You may place the coat flat on a table with the inside of the coat facing upward.
B. Tailor-baste the corresponding pieces of interlining to the wool garment 2 or 3 in. from the seamlines. Baste the armholes.
C. If the *seams were not joined previously*, lap and catch-stitch them, barely catching the wool seams.
D. If the *seams were joined by machine* or *by hand*, attach them to the coat seams by catch-stitching or by permanent basting. An occasional back-stitch will hold the interlining more securely.
E. At the *hemline*, the interlining may be basted to the hemline reinforcement of the sleeve hem and the coat hem. Or, it may be inserted in the lining hems.
F. The interlining may be attached over the *front facing* and catch-stitched, or placed under the raw edge and fastened with a permanent basting on the facing seam allowance.
G. At the *neckline*, attach it by hand to the seam allowance. If there is a back neck facing, trim away the interlining to remove bulk.
H. The *sleeve interlining* may be stitched to the lining cap when a partial sleeve interlining is used. The interlining seam may be trimmed off to reduce bulk or small slashes made and the cut edges lapped. A *full sleeve interlining* may be attached by overlapping the interlining seams of the body of the coat and catch-stitching or permanently basting into position. Another method is to attach the sleeve lining and interlining all the way around before the lining is attached to the armscye.

CHAPTER 30

Constructing and Attaching the Lining

LININGS may be attached to tailored garments before or after the shoulder seams are closed. For most women's fitted garments, it is considered desirable to complete the jacket, press, and then attach the lining by hand. This gives a "custom finish" (Method I).

When tailoring men's sport coats, box jackets, or straight coats, the "floating lining" may be used. In this method, the lining is attached before the shoulder seams are closed, so the garment is laid out flat during the procedure (Method II).

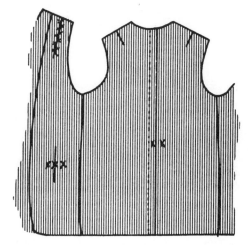

Fig. 247. Constructing the body lining.

Method I. Attaching a Lining by Hand After Completing a Garment

I. Construct the body lining.

A. *Optional:* Stay-stitch the neck and armscye lines.

B. Duplicate the jacket alterations on the lining.

C. Permanently stitch the side seams, all lengthwise seams, and the center back seam of the lining, if there is one. Do not stitch the shoulder seams or the sleeves into the armholes (Fig. 247).

D. Press the seams on the line of stitching. Press the front sleeve seam toward the front. Press the other seams open. Press the darts downward.

E. Baste in a fold or pleat at the center back (Fig. 247).

 1. Be sure the fold or pleat is in the exact center back.

 2. Turn the inside fold to the left side of the garment.

F. Darts may be fastened in before the lining is attached or after it is fitted into the coat (Fig. 247). (The author prefers to baste darts now and catch-stitch later.)

 1. *Darts in coats or peplum jackets* with a waistline seam may be stitched in with the waistline seam.

 2. Fitting darts at the waistline may be catch-stitched at the waistline.

 3. *Large waistline darts* may be stitched in.

 4. *Back shoulder darts* may be stitched in, but *front shoulder darts* are usually catch-stitched part way from the right side of the lining.

II. Fasten the body lining into the coat.

A. The coat is well pressed and turned inside out. It may be placed on a form, on another person, on a hanger, or flat on the table with the wrong

side up. The latter method is preferred by the author.

B. Place the wrong side of the lining
against the wrong side of the coat.

C. Pin the center back of the lining at
the neck edge against the center back
of the coat. Be sure to provide for
seam allowance in the lining. Pin
down the center back to the waistline.

D. Fold back the front lining and match
the underarm seam of the lining to
the corresponding coat seam, attaching together the lining and the garment seam edges which are pressed
toward the front. Permanent-baste
together with long, loose threads,
leaving 2 to 3 in. free at the armscye
and coat bottom. Clip the seams if
they are curved. Do both the right
and left sides (Fig. 248).

E. Place the *front lining* into position.
Check the grain at the bustline. Turn
under the *front edge of the lining*,
lapping over onto the facing, working
from the bustline up and the bustline downward. Baste into position.
The lining will be eased at the bustline (Fig. 249, A) and the hip (Fig.

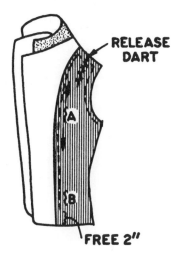

Fig. 249. The lining
basted into position.

249, B), not taut. Check, fold in, and
baste the *release* dart at the shoulder.
Leave the lining free for 2 to 3 in.
at the hemline for a jacket or 4 to
5 in. for a coat.

F. Tailor-baste across the shoulder and
around the armscye about 1 in. from
the seamline. Do not turn under the
front lining at the shoulder seam.
At the *shoulder*, permanent-baste the
seam of the lining to the coat-pad
reinforcement. If you are working
with the garment on a form, turn the
right side out before doing the permanent basting to check the ease of the
lining over the pad (Fig. 249).

G. Place the back of the garment against
the table and pin the grainline of
the lining and garment across the
shoulder blades, working from center back toward armscye (Fig. 250).

H. Smooth the lining into position from
the pinned line up along the armscye
and the neck edge. (The center back
pleat may be adjusted, if needed, for
fitting.) Ease the lining over the
shoulder blades.

I. Clip the curved lining seam at several places almost to the stayline or
the seamline at the neck edge. Turn

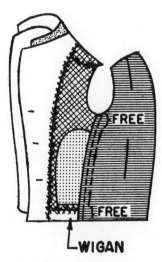

Fig. 248. Fastening the
lining into the coat.

back the seam allowance, pin, and baste the *shoulder seams of the lining* to the shoulder seams of the garment, lapping the back over the front lining (Fig. 250). Pin and baste the

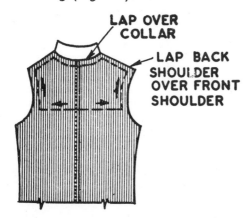

Fig. 250.   The back of the garment.

neck edge of the lining over the raw edge of the top collar at the seamline. If a facing is used at the back neck edge, then the lining is placed onto the bottom edge of the facing.

J. With permanent basting, baste around the entire *armscye seam*, attaching the lining seam to the wool, just outside of the seam, close to the stitching. Under the arms, the backstitch may be used. At the shoulder you will need to stab-stitch through the reinforcement and pads (Fig. 251).

K. Catch-stitch (if not done previously) the *center back pleat* of the lining through the fold for about 1½ in. down from the neckline. Catch-stitch the *front shoulder release dart* about halfway down the dart. The *waistline dart* may be catch-stitched across or for a few stitches lengthwise. Do not catch the wool. On fitted suit coats, the *center back pleat* may be catch-stitched for a few stitches at the bottom of the hem.

L. Using waxed hand-sewing silk, or heavy-duty thread matched to the

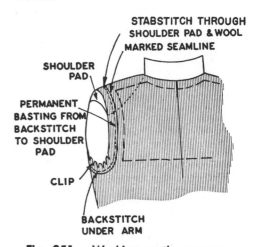

Fig. 251.   Working on the armscye.

wool, slip-stitch the entire lining into position.

III. Baste the lining to the bottom of the coat.

A. Turn up the hem ¾ to 1 in. from the bottom of the coat, depending on the garment. A man's fully lined sport-coat lining is usually ⅜ to ½ in. from the bottom of the coat.

B. Baste evenly 1 to 2 in. from the coat bottom.

C. Fell the lining to the coat (see step IV, C, 1–4 below). See p. 126 for the hem of a full-length coat.

D. Attach the lining to the facing at the bottom where it was left free for 2 to 3 in.

E. Check the lining for length.

IV. Attach the sleeve lining.

A. Turn the sleeve and the lining inside out. Pin and baste the corresponding front side of the sleeve seam to the front side lining seam, matching the notches. Leave 3 in. free at the armscye and 3 in. at the bottom of the sleeve. *Optional:* Repeat for the second seam if there is one. Be sure the lining is somewhat slack, not taut or eased (Fig. 252).

B. Place your hand inside of the lining through the cap end, grasping the

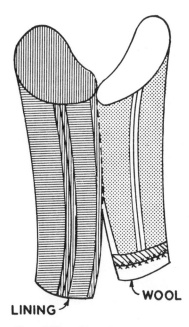

LINING →   ↘ **WOOL**

Fig. 252.   The sleeve lining.

lining and the sleeve at the bottom and pull through. The lining will be right side out over the wool sleeve.

C. Finish the lining at the sleeve bottom.

1. Turn under the raw edge of the lining at the seam allowance.
2. Lap over the edge of the wool hem at least ½ in.
3. Baste back ½ in. from the folded edge.
4. Turn back the folded edge ¼ in. and attach underneath through one thickness of the lining to the wool hem using a running catch stitch. This leaves a tucklike

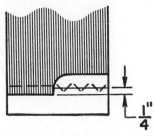

$\frac{1"}{4}$

Fig. 253.   Making the hem.

fold with no felling showing (Fig. 253).

D. *Optional* (this method is used by the tailor when the tucklike fold method, as discussed above, is not used): Baste the lining along the upper edge of the reinforcement of the sleeve bottom with permanent basting. Place the extra length of the lining above this line. This must be invisible from the right side.

E. Run a basting around the sleeve on a filling line about 2 to 4 in. below the lower curve of the armscye (Fig. 254). This basting will be removed later.

F. If the sleeve is lined before it is set into the garment, the sleeve is ready to be set in.

G. Turn under the top of the sleeveline and pin, easing the cap, and baste the entire sleeve lining into place in the armscye of the garment covering the permanent basting around the armscye. Some use a machine or hand gathering thread at the seamline of the sleeve lining which can be pulled up to assist in easing fullness at the cap. Excess fullness in the seam may be removed by notches (Fig. 254).

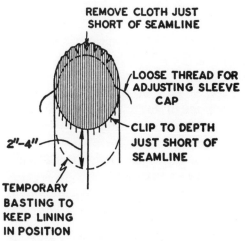

REMOVE CLOTH JUST
SHORT OF SEAMLINE

LOOSE THREAD FOR
ADJUSTING SLEEVE
CAP

CLIP TO DEPTH
JUST SHORT OF
SEAMLINE

2"–4"

TEMPORARY
BASTING TO
KEEP LINING
IN POSITION

Fig. 254.   A second method of attaching the sleeve lining.

H. Fell the lining sleeve seam into position.

Method II. "Floating Lining"— Facing Attached by Machine to the Lining Front

I. Attach the front facing to the lining.
A. Baste the facing and the lining together.
    1. Lay the lining on top of the facing with the right sides together.
    2. Baste from the top down, placing your finger between the lining and the facing, stretching the lining slightly (Fig. 255).
    3. Ease across the bust and toward the waistline (Fig. 255).
    4. Stretch below the waistline (Fig. 255).

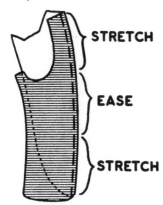

STRETCH

EASE

STRETCH

Fig. 255. Attaching the front facing to the lining.

B. Stitch the seam.
    1. Stitch from the lining side.
    2. Stitch to ½ in. above the seam allowance at the bottom.
C. Press.
    1. Dampen the suit material only, never the lining.
    2. Press the seam toward the lining.

II. Baste the front lining into position. See Chapter 21, step VII, A–C, p. 91.

III. Finish the side seam of the jacket.
A. Baste, check for fit, and stitch the side seams.
B. Press. Do not close the shoulder seams.
C. Clip the seams at the waistline of a fitted garment.

IV. Hem the bottom of the coat (optional at this time for a women's garment).
A. See Chapter 26, p. 108.
B. A reinforcement is rarely used on a man's sport coat.

V. Assemble and prepare the back lining pieces.
A. Stitch the seam allowance at the center back if there is one. Press the seams open.
B. Baste in the darts.
C. Baste the center back pleat with the upper fold of the pleat at the center back.

VI. Fit the back lining to the coat back.
A. Place the coat on the table with the wrong side up, smoothing it evenly.
B. Place the back lining against the coat back, wrong sides together, with the center backs coinciding. Pin into position. Allow for a seam across the neckline.

VII. Prepare and attach the right underarm seam.
A. Lay the back lining over the front and pat it to provide ease. Chalkmark both the front and back seam of the lining directly over the underarm seam of the garment.
B. Baste and stitch the seam, right sides together. Press open. Clip the seam of a fitted garment to within ⅛ in. of the seamline.
C. Permanent-baste the lining and wool seam together, leaving 3 to 4 in. free at the armscye and the top of the coat hem.

VIII. **Prepare and attach the left under-arm seam.**

A. Repeat step VII, A, B, and C, above.

B. When stitching and attaching the seam, turn the right sides of the lining together. The body of the coat will be between the left lining forepart and the back lining.

C. NOTE: On men's sport coats, the lining and coat seams are sometimes left loose.

IX. **Turn the coat to the inside.**

Turn it as you would a glove so that the seams of the lining are facing the coat seams.

X. **Baste the back lining.**

A. Pat the lining with your hands to allow for ease in the back.

B. Baste with tailor basting from A–B and C–D in Figure 256 keeping 3 in. in from seams.

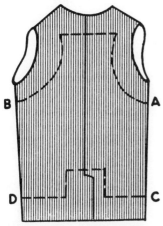

Fig. 256. Basting the back lining.

XI. **Baste the lining to the bottom of the coat.**

A. See Method I, III, A–D, above.

B. In a man's sport coat with a back vent, clip the lining to baste at an angle from A to B in Figure 257. Fell the lining from A to B and to the wool on the overlap and underlap of the vent.

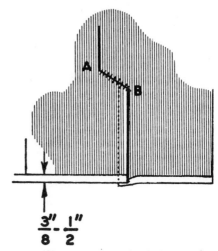

$$\frac{3''}{8} - \frac{1''}{2}$$

Fig. 257. Basting the lining to the bottom of the coat.

XII. **Stitch and press the shoulder seams of the garment.**

A. See Chapter 20, p. 87.

B. On a man's sport coat, complete the shoulder-lining seam as in Method I, I, p. 121. When felling the lining seam, be sure that the interfacings are not caught.

C. The neck edge of the lining is left raw and the top collar is sewed over it. Baste the raw neck edge of the lining into position, tacking the center back pleat into position.

XIII. **Put on the collar.**

See Chapter 22, p. 92; Chapter 23, p. 96; or Chapter 24, p. 99.

XIV. **Attach the sleeve lining.**

See Method I, step IV, A–H, p. 122.

XV. **Stitch in the sleeves.**

See Chapter 25, p. 102.

XVI. **Attach the pads.**

See Chapter 25, p. 107.

XVII. **Attach the lining to the shoulder and the neckline edges.**

A. See Method I, step II, F–K, p. 121.

B. Omit this step for a man's sport coat.

XVIII. **Attach the sleeve lining.**

See Method I, step IV, G–H, p. 123.

Hemming the Lining of Outer Coats

I. Hang the lining hem.
A. Try on the garment and have some-one pin the lining to the garment about 8–10 in. from the bottom of the coat, or
B. Hang the garment on a hanger or form and do likewise.

II. Turn up the hem and baste.
A. After hemming, the lining should be ¾–1 in. shorter than the coat hem.
B. The lining hem may be as wide as the coat hem or slightly narrower.

III. Put up the lining hem.
A. Construct the hem as a skirt hem.
B. See p. 149.
C. Attach the lining to the facing at the bottom where it was left free for 4 to 5 in.

IV. Attach the lining hem to the coat.
A. Swing-tack the lining to the coat at the seamlines at the top of the coat hem.
B. See p. 37 for directions for making a swing tack.

Zip-Out Lining

NOTE: Check to be sure that the back neck facing of the coat and the front facing are the same width. If not, cut them the same width and adjust the lining accordingly.

I. Complete the coat except for inserting the lining.

II. Attach the zipper to the coat facing. (The lining usually zips from right to left.)
A. Bind the inside edge of the coat facing with a matching bias tape.
B. Match the center marking of a sep-arating zipper (about 80 in.) to the center back neck facing with the zipper face up.

C. Place the bound edge of the facing on top of the zipper, extending the edge about ¼ in. beyond the zipper teeth. Using a zipper foot, stitch the inner edge of the zipper tape to the facing. Stitch through the tape and the facing only.

III. Complete the lining (Fig. 258, a).
A. Fit the lining to the coat, pinning the lining to the coat at the armscye edges and the side seams.

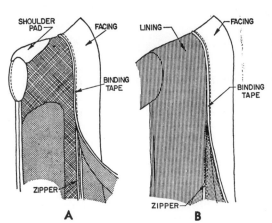

Fig. 258.   Making a zip-out lining.

B. Lap the front and neck edges of the lining over the free edge of the zipper tape. Turn under the excess lining. Trim the excess lining and clip the zipper tape so that it fits the curve smoothly (Fig. 258, b).

IV. Attach the lining to the zipper.
A. Separate the zipper.
B. Using a zipper foot, stitch the lining to the zipper tape. Stitch the entire length of the zipper.

V. Complete the zip-out lining.
A. You may sew snaps at the armhole and side seams to connect the lining and the coat at the shoulders.
B. Snaps or loops and buttons may be sewed at the bottom of the sleeve edge to connect the sleeve lining to the coat.
C. Hem the lining to the desired length.

CHAPTER 31

Final Pressing of a Garment

THE final pressing of a garment is done after the lining is in and the garment is finished except for the buttons. Leave in the center front guidelines. An excellent job of steaming many times covers up defective workmanship and helps give the garment that "custom-made" appearance. Many amateurs prefer to take their garment to a tailor or dry-cleaning establishment for this pressing. Be sure to tell them to hand-press and shape the garment or to press it on an adjustable form where it is steamed first and the nap raised with cold air.

I. Press the body of the garment.

A. Press the lined garment on the right side, using proper press cloths (see Chapter 8, p. 38).

B. Double surfaces should be pressed on both sides, as revers, collar, and front facing.

C. See Chapter 27, steps II–VI, p. 112, for the pressing technique.

II. Press the lining.

A. Some lining fabrics water spot; therefore care must be taken not to drop water on the lining.

B. Press the lining with the coat fabric against the ironing board and the lining side up.

C. Use a warm iron. You may use a dry press cloth.

D. Press a crease in the lining at the center back pleat, at the bottom hem, and where it is attached to facing.

E. Turn the sleeve wrong side out and press it on a sleeve board. Press a crease in the hem, then press upward. At the cap, place the end over the end of the sleeve board to remove wrinkles.

III. Allow the garment to dry.

A. Dry the garment flat on a table.

B. Hang on a hanger.

CHAPTER 32

Attaching Buttons

AFTER completing the final pressing of the garment, the buttons are attached. If the garment is to fit well, the buttons must be located properly and attached by the correct method.

The buttons used on a tailored garment may be self-covered or of bone, pearl, plastic, or similar material. They may have a shank or holes through them. Buttons vary in size according to the style and type of the garment, the weight of the material, and the fashion trends. Generally for a man's suit coat, No. 30 (¾-in. diameter) are used for the front and No. 25 (⅝-in. diameter) for the sleeve. On children's garments it is better to use a larger button to make it easier for them to fasten their own garments. Button sizes for coats are as follows:

No. 36 — ⅞-in. diameter ⎫
No. 40 — 1 -in. diameter ⎬ Topcoat
No. 45 — 1⅛-in diameter ⎭
No. 50 — 1¼-in. diameter ⎫
No. 55 — 1⅜-in. diameter ⎪
No. 60 — 1½-in. diameter ⎬ Overcoat
No. 70 — 1¾-in. diameter ⎭

I. **Mark the positions for the buttons.**

A. Try on the garment, lapping the center front markings directly over one another. On women's garments, lap the right front over the left. Reverse this for men's garments. Be sure the coat buttons are properly aligned.

B. Mark the positions of the buttons with a pin or basting at the end near the outer edge of the button-hole. This marking usually falls on the center front line. Be sure that the

edge of the button is at least ⅓ to ½ in. from the edge of the coat (Fig. 259A).

Fig. 259A. Marking the position of a button.

C. On a man's suit coat the bottom button is about 1½ in. from the sleeve bottom. The centers of the buttons are ⅝ to ¾ in. apart and ⅝ to ¾ in. from the seam (Fig. 259B).

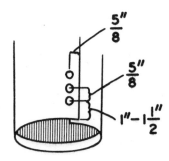

$\frac{5''}{8}$

$\frac{5''}{8}$

$1'' - 1\frac{1}{2}''$

Fig. 259B. Sleeve buttons.

II. **Prepare the thread for sewing on the button.**

A. Linen thread or button thread to match the garment is the most satisfactory for garments receiving hard wear.

B. Matching buttonhole twist, heavy-duty or silk thread may be substituted. Wax with beeswax.

C. Use a double thread.

III. Sew on the button.

A. Button with holes.

1. Secure the thread by inserting the needle between the facing and coat about ¾ in. from the button position leaving a little end extended. At the button position take two or three tiny stitches to anchor the thread. If the cloth is loosely woven, you may use a small knot and draw it between the facing and the coat.

2. Bring the needle up through one of the holes to the top and back through a different hole to the underneath side of the garment.

3. Insert a pin, pencil, or match in the loop of the thread to form a shank (Fig. 260); or the shank

Fig. 260. Forming a shank.

should be as long as the thickness of the coat and the facing.

4. Continue sewing until enough strands are present for durability.

5. Bring the thread up under the button. Remove the pin, match, or the like, pull the button up,

and wind the thread between the button and the fabric to form the shank or "neck." This should be firm and even.

6. Fasten the thread on the wrong side with several small stitches. Cut off the thread.

B. Button with shank.

1. See step II, A, B, and C, above.
2. See step III, A, 1, above.
3. Turn the shank to one side.
4. Sew back and forth through the shank and the cloth, keeping the stitches parallel to the edge of the garment. This places the strain on the shank (Fig. 261).

Fig. 261. Button with shank.

5. A partial thread shank may be needed if the shank of the button is not sufficient.

6. See step III, A, 6, above.

C. Stay button.

1. Tailored garments receiving hard wear have a small button (stay) placed directly underneath the top button on the facing side. This is also good for loosely woven materials.

2. See step III, A, 1–6, above.

3. Both buttons are sewed on in one operation (Fig. 262).

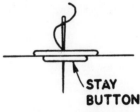

Fig. 262. A stay button.

CHAPTER 33

Other Construction Problems

Constructing a Fly Front for a Coat

A FLY front closing is frequently used on the following tailored garments: sport coats, rain coats, car coats, and boys' topcoats. The buttonholes are concealed under the front edges as are the buttons when the garment is worn closed. The length of the fly varies. Sometimes it begins below the revers and continues down to a few inches below the hip, or it may extend the full length of the garment.

Before constructing the fly facing, the interfacing, taping, and pad-stitching should be completed. The side on which the fly front is placed depends on whether it is a ladies' or men's garment. The fly is on the left for the men and reverse for the ladies.

I. Cut and mark the fly fronts.

A. Use a pattern for the facing and the buttonhole location.
B. Mark the seamlines in the fly facings, coat front, and front facing.
C. Mark carefully the termination points of the fly on both facings and the front coat facing.
D. To avoid bulk, both of the fly facings are sometimes made of lining materials, or just the fly facing which is attached to the coat front.

II. Apply the fly facing to the coat front.

A. Place the fly-facing strip on top of the coat front, right sides together, with the termination points coinciding.

B. Baste and stitch between A and B in Figure 265 on the marked seamline which is the edge of the seam tape.
C. Clip the seam allowance to A and B in Figure 265 at an angle.

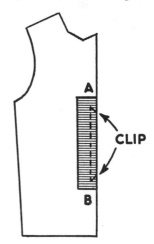

Fig. 265. Applying the fly facing.

D. Press the seam open on an edge presser. Trim and grade the seams. Trim the coat seam to ¼ in. and the facing seam to ⅛ in.
E. Turn to the wrong side of the coat, rolling the seam edge slightly toward the underneath side.
F. Baste and press.

III. Apply the fly facing to the coat facing.

A. This side of the fly facing may be interlined with wigan, silesia, hymo, or muslin, as the buttonholes are made through this strip.

B. The interlining may be cut the same size as the facing and the two basted together and treated as one; or

C. Interlining may be cut the size of the facing strip minus the seam allowances. Then fell the facing seam allowances on three sides (Fig. 266).

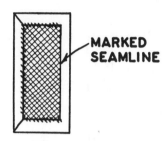

Fig. 266. Felling the facing seam allowances.

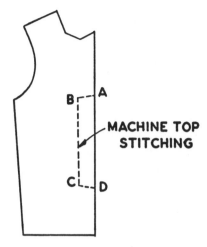

Fig. 267. Top stitching the fly facing.

D. Place the fly-facing strip on the front coat facing, right sides together. Then baste and stitch as in step II, B–F, above.

IV. **Work the buttonholes on the fly and coat facing.**

A. Work the buttonholes on the marked lines through the coat facing, interfacing, and fly facing.

B. See Chapter 28, p. 114.

V. **Apply the coat facing to the coat.**

A. See Chapter 21, p. 89.

B. Begin at A in Figure 265 and proceed to the point at which the collar is attached. Begin at B and proceed to the coat bottom.

VI. **Top-stitch the fly facing.**

A. Top-stitch the fly-facing strips and the coat from the top side from A to B to C to D in Figure 267.

B. This stitching secures the garment, the facing, and the two fly facings together.

VII. **Tack the fly fronts.**

A. Use matching buttonhole twist or heavy-duty or silk thread to tack between the buttonholes.

B. This holds the fly and the front edge together.

Constructing a Back Vent on a Man's Sport Coat

I. Stitch and press open the center back seam.

This seam is usually 1 in. wide and is not trimmed. Do not stitch the vent opening.

II. Chalk a line on the vent to coincide with the stitching line.

III. Tape the left back opening.

A. Place the edge of the tape on the chalked line from the bottom of the vent to ¾ in. above the vent opening.

B. Baste, pulling taut about ⅛ in.

C. Stitch the tape ¼ in. from the chalked fold-seam line. Turn back the taped edge (Fig. 268).

D. Clip the seam and press open.

E. Turn back the other vent edge (right back) ¼ in. and catch-stitch loosely.

F. Baste the vent closed into position.

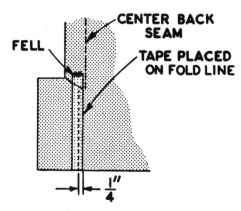

Fig. 268. Basting the vent.

Constructing an Unlined Jacket

An unlined coat should be constructed of firm material, because it has little reinforcement. A coat with straight lines, loosely fitted, and with patch pockets is desirable.

I. Prepare the fabric.
　　See Chapter 6, p. 20.

II. Cut, mark, and stay.
　A. See Chapter 9, p. 41.
　B. Omit cutting the lining.
　C. Cut the interfacing the same as the front facing.

III. Prepare for the first fitting.
　　See Chapter 12, p. 55.

IV. Fit and mark.
　　See Chapter 13, p. 56.

V. Stitch the darts and seams comprising the front and the back.
　A. See Chapter 10, p. 46.
　B. It is better to leave darts uncut in an unlined garment. If they are slashed, they should be bound.
　C. Plain seams are best pressed open and single edge bound. Armscye seams are bound together. Flat fell or welt seams are appropriate for some fabrics (see Chapter 10, p. 48).

VI. Construct the pockets.
　A. Patch pockets are a better choice for unlined garments.
　B. See Chapter 14, p. 70, "Patch Pocket."

VII. Apply the interfacing to the coat.
　A. Use a soft interfacing or lightweight canvas.
　B. See Chapter 16, p. 76.

VIII. Pad-stitch the lapel and the creaseline.
　　See Chapter 17, p. 78.

IX. Trim the interfacing and tape the front edges.
　　See Chapter 18, p. 80.

X. Prepare the bound buttonholes.
　　See Chapter 19, p. 82.

XI. Stitch the side and shoulder seams.
　　See Chapter 20, p. 87, and step V, above.

XII. Attach the front facing.
　A. See Chapter 21, p. 89.
　B. The raw edges of the front facing and the interfacing may be bound together.
　C. Sometimes, in a lightweight fabric, the interfacing is trimmed back and the facing is turned back and self-stitched.

XIII. Prepare and attach the collar.
　A. See Chapter 22, p. 92; Chapter 23, p. 96; or Chapter 24, p. 99.
　B. Usually the machine method of applying the collar and self-material is used.
　C. Since there is no lining to cover the raw edge at the back neckline seam, this seam allowance is clipped and turned under.

D. If a back neck facing is used, join the facing to upper collar, and the undercollar to the neck seam. Clip and press the seams open and permanent-baste together at the seamline.

XIV. Shape and construct the sleeves.

A. See Chapter 25, p. 102.

B. Bind the sleeve seam edges together.

XV. Hem the garment.

A. See Chapter 26, p. 108.

B. Often the hem is not interfaced. If it is, the interfacing may not extend over the hem.

C. Use seam tape to finish the hem. You may apply it flat or bind the edge, then hand-stitch it to the coat.

XVI. Press the garment.

See Chapter 27, p. 112.

CHAPTER **34**

Constructing a Skirt for the First Fitting

Cutting, Marking, Staying, and Preparing for the First Fitting

IF A suit is being tailored, the skirt is cut, marked, and stay-stitched at the same time as the jacket. The skirt has to be prepared as follows for the first fitting.

I. Cut out the pieces for the skirt.
A. Skirt.
    1. Cut out the pieces, on the grain, following the pattern, allowing for adjustments which were made during fitting of the pattern.
    2. Cut the notches beyond the seam (Fig. 271).

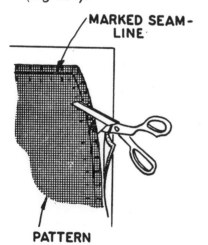

MARKED SEAM-LINE

PATTERN

Fig. 271. Cutting out the skirt.

B. Lining.
    1. Skirts are lined if they are con-structed of loosely woven cloth, are straight in design, or if the wearer has large hips.
    2. Taffeta or a nonstretch rayon crepe which blends in color with the wool may be used.
    3. The lining should extend well down over the hip when the wearer is sitting down. To prevent the side seams from pulling to the back, the front may also be lined.
    4. Cut the lining from the skirt pattern tissue. The selvage at the lower edge of the lining may be used.

C. Belt.
    1. Cut the belt the desired width, plus two seam allowances. The length is the waistline measure plus 3 in. This allows for seams.
    2. Cut the interfacing of hymo or wigan, the same length as the belt except that the width is the finished width of belt plus one seam allowance.

II. Transfer the markings from pattern onto the cloth.
A. Mark the following with tracing wheel or tailor tacks:
    1. Pleats.
    2. Darts.
    3. Tucks.
    4. Gathers.
    5. Pocket location.
    6. Any other construction details.
B. Remove the pattern tissue.

III. Stay-stitch the skirt pieces.

A. At the waistline, stitch ½ in. from the cut edge, beginning at the side seam and stitching toward the center front or back. Do this to all the waistline edges of the pieces which comprise the front and back of the skirt (Fig. 272).

B. On the side seams, stay-stitch ¼ to ⅜ in. from the edge from the end of zipper to the waistline on both sides (Fig. 272).

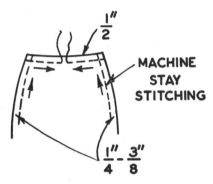

Fig. 272. Stay-stitching the skirt pieces.

IV. Baste up the skirt.

A. Baste in the darts.

See Chapter 10, step II, G, p. 46; step IV, A and B, p. 47; step V, A–C, p. 47; step VI, A–D, p. 47; step VII, A and B, p. 47; and step VIII, A–E, p. 48.

B. Baste in the pleats.

1. Pleats set in from the wrong side. Pleats may be set in from the wrong side, by matching the marked lines of each pleat. Be sure the pleats are turned in the direction in which they are to be pressed. This method does not leave thread imprints when pressing; or

2. Pleats set in from the right side. Pleats may be set in from the right side. Edge-baste the fold of

each pleat, and pin it into position. Baste. Press. Remove the edge bastings and press again to remove the thread imprints.

3. Pleats set in with the seam at the back edge. On the right side, place the folded edge of the pleat to the proper line. Smooth out the layers underneath, then baste underneath the seam.

C. Baste the side seams.

1. The side seams may be machine-basted or hand-basted.

2. Use directional basting, or you may, as many tailors do, baste down on the right side and up on the left.

3. Press along the basting line.

D. Stitch the interfacing onto the belt.

1. Press the belt in half lengthwise. Be careful not to stretch, but, rather, ease in the folded edge.

2. Stitch the interfacing ⅛ to ¼ in. below the foldline onto the half of the band which lies nearer the wearer when attached to the skirt (Fig. 273).

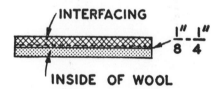

Fig. 273. Stitching the interfacing onto the belt.

E. Shape the interfaced belt.

1. From the side seam to the ends of the belt, using a circular motion, stretch the cut edges slightly,

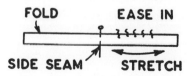

Fig. 274. Shaping the belt.

easing in on the folded edge (Fig. 274).

2. Repeat for the other half of the belt.

F. Fit, mark, and baste the skirt belt onto the skirt.

1. Place the right side of the front belt against the right side of the front skirt with the belt extending about 1 in. over the placket opening (Fig. 275).
2. Place a pin at the center front (Fig. 275).
3. Measure one half of the waistline; measure on the belt from the cen-

CENTER BACK

CENTER FRONT

MACHINE TOP STITCHING FOR ZIPPER

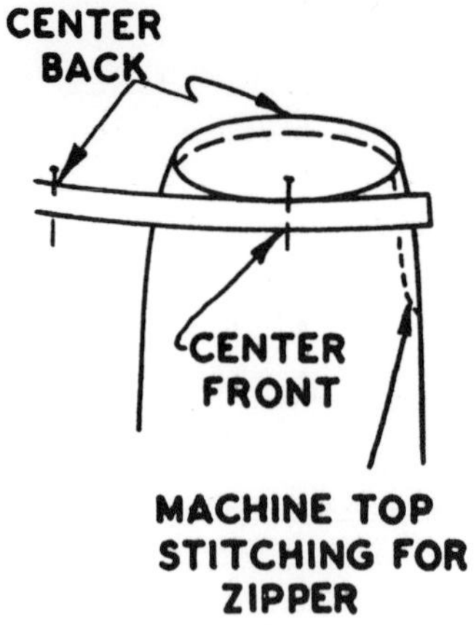

Fig. 275. Attaching the belt to the skirt.

ter front toward the center back, and place another pin which then marks the center back (Fig. 275). (For example, if the waistline measure is 24 in., measure 12 in.)

4. Pin the center back of the belt to the center back of the skirt (Fig. 275).
5. The skirt will be eased onto the belt over the front hipbone and the side back.
6. Fold back the loose ends (both front and back) and measure to the side seams for equal distances and pin the halves of the belt into position. There will be loose ends of the belt extending over both the front and back of the placket opening during the first fitting.
7. Fold the belt over and baste the inside edge down flat without turning it under.

At This Point, the Skirt Is Ready for the First Fitting

V. Check the fit.

A. See Chapter 41, p. 154, "The Skirt."
B. Make necessary alterations and refit if needed.
C. Mark the seam positions on the band.

CHAPTER **35**

Constructing Pleats and Darts in a Skirt

PLEATS in a tailored garment add fullness and/or are decorative in effect. Fashion often dictates as to the type, length, location, and number of pleats. Pleats are best in firm cloth that will hold a sharp crease. The types of pleats most commonly used on tailored garments are *side (knife) pleats* and *box pleats*. The latter type may be *inverted*.

See Chapter 10, p. 46, for a discussion of the marking, stitching, and pressing of darts.

Pleats

I. Types of pleats.

A. Side pleat.

1. A side (knife) pleat is a pleat with a folded edge turned in one direction. It may be used singly or in groups, all turned in one direction (Fig. 278).

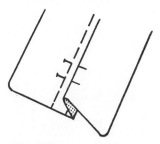

Fig. 278. A side pleat.

2. Sometimes the back edge of a side pleat may fall into a seam, or it may be cut as an extension on each side of a seam. Do not press the seam open.

B. Box pleat.

1. This pleat is formed by two pleats in opposite directions with the folded edges meeting on the underneath side of the pleat (Fig. 279).

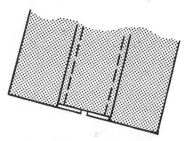

Fig. 279. A box pleat.

2. The pleat is usually twice the width of the two side pleats from which it is composed.

C. Inverted pleat.

1. Inverted pleats may be set in a seam, or made with an inlay or from extensions cut on from the garment.

2. Follow the pattern instructions for the procedure.

II. Mark and baste in the pleats.

A. See Chapter 34, step IV, B, 1-3, p. 135.

B. If many pleats are made, the skirt may be placed with the warp grain lengthwise on an ironing board. Lay

137

the pleats in place and pin them to the board, then press. This eliminates basting along the foldline (Fig. 280).

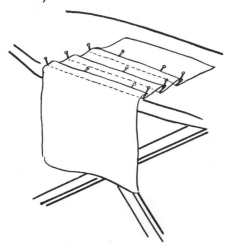

Fig. 280.   Pinning the pleats.

C. When pinning pleats, pin at right angles to the folded pleat edge.
D. A cardboard gauge may be useful in measuring many pleats so they will be uniform in size.

III. Stitch the pleats.
A. A basting or the edge of the presser foot may be used as a guide when stitching pleats by machine.

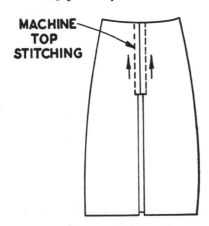

Fig. 281.   Stitching the pleats.

B. Stitch across the lower end *first*, then up to the waistline. Begin the other edge at the bottom and stitch to the waistline also. This method keeps the grain in line (Fig. 281).
C. Pull the threads to the wrong side. Tie them in a square knot and cut the threads, leaving about ½ to 1 in.
D. Pleats may be stitched in various ways. A handworked arrowhead or crow's-foot may also be placed at the end of a pleat (Fig. 282).

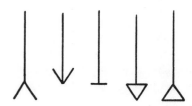

Fig. 282.   Pleat ideas.

E. Wool or blends which are washable may have the pleat edges edge-stitched and back edge of each pleat stitched.
F. If the pleats do not extend to the waistline, they ought to be stitched across the top to support the under layers.
G. To remove excess bulk at the waistline seam in heavy material, stitch

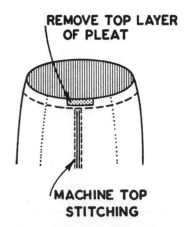

Fig. 283.   Removing excess bulk in the waist seam.

by machine through the skirt and the pleats. Trim off the pleats just above the stitching line. The stitching line will be covered by the belt (Fig. 283).

IV. Check the pleats for proper hanging.
A. Stay the pleats to keep them from spreading.
 1. To keep the pleats from spreading without stitching, particularly around the upper hip area, place a piece of lining fabric behind them.
 2. Sometimes a nonstretch tape is used and is caught to the back edge of each pleat.
B. Stay the underseam to keep it from stretching.
 1. If the seam on the back edge of a pleat is not on the straight grain,

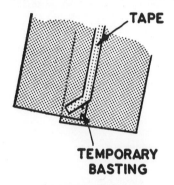

Fig. 284. Taping the underseam.

it may stretch. This will cause the pleat to hang out.
 2. Pin tape on the seam. Try on the skirt to check the hang of the pleat (Fig. 284).
 3. Stitch through the tape and the seam.
C. Stay the folded edge to prevent stretching.
 1. If the folded edge is not on the straight grain, this may stretch.
 2. Place seam binding ribbon or linen tape with one edge along the foldline and the other edge toward the inner side of the pleat.
 3. Pin the tape slightly taut. Try on to check the hang.
 4. Hand-hem the tape so it is invisible from the right side.
D. Pleats that swing outward.
 Pull the pleat up slightly at the back edge to correct this difficulty.

V. Press.
A. Press the pleats, being careful not to stretch the folded edge.
B. Mark the hemline, turn up the hem, and lightly press the bottom of the hem to mark the inside fold of the pleats.
C. Remove bastings to release the pleats. The marking will be continuous.
D. Press to reverse the direction of the pleatline through the hem allowance.

CHAPTER **36**

Constructing Skirt Seams and Lining a Skirt

AFTER pressing the darts and pleats, re-baste the side seams according to the alterations made during the first fitting.

A skirt lining may be partial, that is just the back of the skirt lined, or both the back and the front may be lined. The lining may fall below the hip or to the hemline. It may be stitched into the seams as an underlining or be complete and separate from the skirt and attached at the waistline.

I. Stitch the seams.

A. Plain seams are most generally used.

B Heavier fabrics require a looser tension and longer stitch than light-weight fabrics.

C. For stretchy fabrics use a light tension, so the seams will stretch with the cloth. Treat bias or semibias skirt gorelines in the same manner.

D. The tailor stitches the right seam from the top to the bottom and the left side from the bottom to the top. (Dressmakers use directional stitching, stitching from the bottom to the top on both sides) (Fig. 287).

E. Be sure to stitch straight. A machine gauge is helpful.

II. Remove the bastings and press.

A. Press the seams open by holding the allowances open with the fingers on

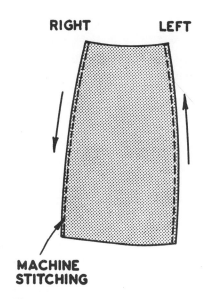

RIGHT   LEFT

MACHINE
STITCHING

Fig. 287.   Stitching the seams.

the left hand, and follow the stitching line with the point of the iron. This gives an inconspicuous line.

B. Press the seams in the direction in which they were stitched.

C. If a seamline is to be emphasized, press both edges in one direction.

D. The side seams and the area along the side seam from the waist to the hipline must not be stretched. The seamline may be pressed open on an edge presser or a seam board, and then pressed over a tailor's cushion.

Be sure to shrink in the rippled outer edges of the seam allowances (Fig. 288).

TAILOR'S HAM

Fig. 288. Pressing the seams. For purposes of clarity the press cloth is not shown.

E. If the material leaves seam imprints, then press the seam open on an edge presser or a padded roll.
F. Strips of brown paper placed under the seam allowances will also prevent imprints.
G. Flatten the seams with a beater (clapper).

III. Finish the seam edges.

A. Edges of seams which ravel may be overcast. Other accepted finishes are to bind the edges with silk or rayon bias binding, or to stitch seam binding flat on both raw edges of the seam (Fig. 289).

B. Fabrics that do not ravel may be left plain or the edges may be pinked (Fig. 289).
C. An automatic zigzag machine or zigzag attachment may be used to finish raw edges (Fig. 289).

IV. Attach the lining or underlining.

A. A partial lining (back only) may be attached to the skirt seams by hand before the belt is attached, or it may be stitched into the seams. If the skirt lining is to be stitched into the side seams, baste the lining with the side seams, making the lining slightly taut. (The lining seams will be about ¹⁄₁₆ to ⅛ in. wider than the skirt seam on each side.) Allow the placket edge to remain free.
B. A separate lining is attached at the waistline after the placket (zipper) is completed and is not attached at the seams.
C. The darts and seams are placed toward the skirt with the darts turned in the opposite direction to the skirt darts to avoid bulk.
D. In unpressed pleats, the lining and wool are folded together in one operation.
E. In a full-length lining where there is a pleat, slash the lining (Fig. 290) at the top of the pleat. Place that

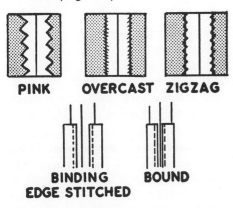

PINK OVERCAST ZIGZAG

BINDING BOUND
EDGE STITCHED

Fig. 289. Finishing the seam edges.

LINING IS TRIMMED TO ³⁄₈" FROM STITCHING LINE

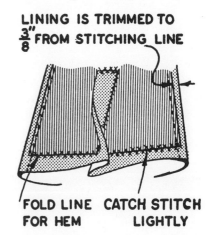

FOLD LINE CATCH STITCH
FOR HEM LIGHTLY

Fig. 290. Attaching the lining.

portion of the lining under the pleat and hand-sew lightly. Catch-stitch the lining across the top of the pleat and along the top side of the pleat.

F. The *bottom* of a *below-the-hip lining* may be cut on a selvage; otherwise, the raw edge is pinked, turned under once, and self-stitched near the edge by machine.

G. The *bottom* of a full-length underlining sewed into the seams may be catch-stitched lightly inside the hem at the foldline.

H. The *bottom* of a full-length lining which is separate is fastened at the bottom after the hem is in. It may be attached the same as the lining at the bottom of a sleeve. See Figure 253, p. 123. Sometimes it is left free and self-stitched at a length even with the top of the hem.

NOTE: After the zipper is inserted, lap the lining over the edges of the tape and hand-hem firmly. This gives a smooth finish covering the seam edges.

CHAPTER 37

Applying a Zipper to a Skirt

A ZIPPER is the most commonly accepted type of closure used today for skirt-placket openings. It is interesting to note that although the inception of the idea of the first sliding fastener originated at the end of the nineteenth century, it wasn't until 1923 that zippers were widely used in clothing.

In a skirt, although zippers are usually set into a side-seam placket, sometimes they are set into a center back seam. In the latter method, the zipper is inserted with two folds meeting over the metal. Both methods will be discussed.

Zipper Set Into a Side-Seam Placket

I. Parts of a zipper.

The parts of the zipper are: cord, top-stop scoops (teeth), automatic lock slider, pull tab, twill tape, chain, and bottom stop (Fig. 293).

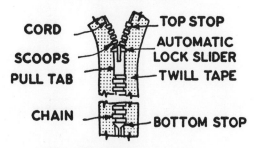

CORD

SCOOPS

PULL TAB

CHAIN

TOP STOP

AUTOMATIC LOCK SLIDER

TWILL TAPE

BOTTOM STOP

Fig. 293. Parts of a zipper.

II. Select a zipper of the proper weight and length.

A. Use a medium-heavy zipper (about ¼ in. wide) for sports jackets, heavy tweeds, etc.

B. Use a medium-lightweight zipper (about ¾₁₆ in. wide) for lightweight wool suits.

C. Use a still lighter weight zipper for sheer wool.

D. A usual length of a skirt zipper is 7 in.; however, sometimes a 9-in. is used, or in some suits with short jackets, two short zippers are used. One is placed on each side of the skirt.

E. Automatic lock sliders allow the zipper to lock wherever it stops.

F. A skirt-placket zipper is closed at the bottom and open at the top.

III. Points to check before applying the zipper.

A. Be sure the skirt is fitted properly, and all seams are finished and pressed.

B. Place the zipper in the *left* side seam or the center back seam.

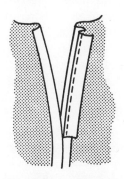

Fig. 294. Attaching the zipper.

C. When measuring for the placket opening, measure from the top stop to the bottom stop of the zipper plus the waistline seam allowance. Keep the zipper taut when measuring.

D. If the seam allowance of the placket is less than ⅝ in., stitch seam binding, a selvage strip of fabric, belting ribbon, or grosgrain to the front edge of seam allowance (Fig. 294).

IV. Machine-baste the placket opening.

A. Use a long machine stitch, stitching from the bottom of the skirt placket to the top (Fig. 295).

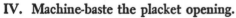
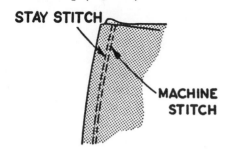
STAY STITCH

MACHINE STITCH

Fig. 295. Making the placket opening.

B. The basting stitch may be clipped at 2- to 3-in. intervals for ease of removal.

C. Press the seam open.

V. Attach the zipper to the back seam allowance.

A. Put a zipper or cording foot on the sewing machine. Adjust the machine-stitching to regulation stitch.

B. Open the zipper.

C. Place the zipper face down on the back seam allowance with the edge of the scoops (teeth) at the seamline. The bottom stop will be at the end of the basting (Fig. 296, a).

D. Stitch it to the seam allowance next to the zipper, beginning above the pull tab at the hip end of the placket and stitch up to the waist. Ease the fabric to the zipper tape (Fig. 296, a).

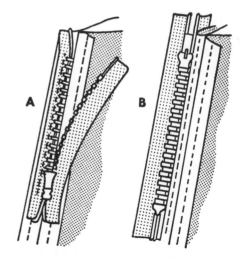

Fig. 296. Attaching the zipper to the back seam allowance.

E. Close the zipper, turning it face up. Be sure the pull tab is up. Turn back the seam allowance at the zipper edge, creasing it slightly. Stitch from the end of the twill tape at the bottom to the top, and stitch close to the cloth edge, about 1/16 in. (Fig. 296, b).

VI. Attach the zipper to the front of the garment.

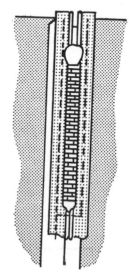

Fig. 297. Attaching the zipper to the front.

A. Place the zipper face down, so that it is flat on the seam.

B. Stitch across the lower ends of the zipper, and up the front seam allowance next to the chain, up to the top of the skirt (Fig. 297).

C. Keep the pull tab up when stitching.

D. To turn a sharp corner, raise the presser foot and pivot on the needle with the needle in the fabric. Then lower the presser foot and continue stitching.

E. Fan out the stitching slightly around the slider and the pull tab.

   NOTE: (Hand Method) Steps B through C may be done by hand using a tiny back stitch. The thread floats on the top should appear as tiny pricks.

VII. Finish and press.

A. Press the closure from the right side of the garment.

B. Place a towel on the ham or pressing mitt with the inside of the garment against it.

C. Use a moistened press cloth over the closure and hold the iron lightly over the placket. Allow the steam to penetrate. If the cloth is lightweight, place paper between the chain and the cloth to avoid marks. Press from the waist to the hip. Do not press over the metal fastener from the wrong side. Allow it to dry.

D. Remove the machine basting.

Zipper Set Into a Center Back Seam

I.–IV. See steps I to IV above.

V. Attach the zipper to one side of the seam allowance.

A. Place the zipper or cording foot on the machine.

B. Open the zipper, placing it face down on the seam allowance with the edge of the scoops (teeth) along the seamline and the bottom stop at the end of the basting (see step V, above).

C. Stitch next to the metal zipper, beginning at the top of the pull tab at the hip end and stitch to the waist.

VI. Attach the zipper on both sides.

A. Close the zipper with its center face down on the seamline.

B. Stitch down on the side which was previously stitched, across the end, and up the other side (Fig. 298).

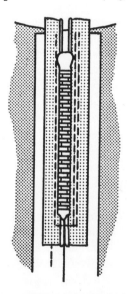

Fig. 298. Attaching the zipper on both sides.

C. If the material is a check or plaid, you may stitch both sides in the same direction to keep them in line.

VII. See step VII above.

CHAPTER **38**

Applying the Skirt Belt

AFTER the zipper is applied and the skirt is pressed, you are ready to attach the skirt belt. The lining should be secured at the zipper tape at this time. See Chapter 36, step IV, I, p. 142. The skirt belt was shaped, lined, and fitted during the first fitting of the garment.

I. Close the ends of the belt.

A. If hooks and eyes close the front belt end along the seamline, an underlap may be left at the back. This gives a flat, inconspicuous closing.

B. If a button closure is to be used, make a buttonhole (see Chapter 19, p. 82; Chapter 28, p. 114) on the front overlap. If a bound buttonhole is used, make it before the end of the belt is closed. Worked buttonholes are made after the belt is completed and attached to the skirt. The button is sewed on the underlap.

C. Stitch the ends of the belt with the right sides together, and the strip folded on the lengthwise crease. On the belt end which has the extension, continue stitching along the waistline to the point where it is to be matched to the skirt (Fig. 301).

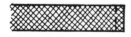

EXTENSION

Fig. 301. Belt end extension.

D. Trim the seam allowances to ⅛ to ¼ in., grading the edges of the cloth if bulky and skive at the corners of the belt. Turn the belt right side out and press.

E. Clip the seam allowance on the inside of the belt (the side toward the wearer) (Fig. 302).

INSIDE OF BELT

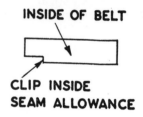

**CLIP INSIDE
SEAM ALLOWANCE**

Fig. 302. Clipping the belt.

F. Shape the belt once more before applying it to the skirt (see Chapter 34, step IV, E, p. 135).

II. Attach the belt to the skirt.

A. Baste the belt onto the skirt.
Use the markings as determined during the first fitting for applying the skirt belt (see Chapter 34, step IV, F, 1–5, p. 136) (Fig. 303).

B. Machine-stitch the belt to the skirt.
1. Place the skirt side down when stitching.
2. Backstitch at the ends.
3. Grade the seam allowances of the belt to ⅜ in. and the skirt seam allowance to ¼ in. Turn them into the belt. Clip if necessary. Press the seamline.

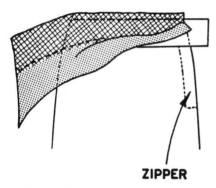

ZIPPER

Fig. 303. Attaching the belt to the skirt.

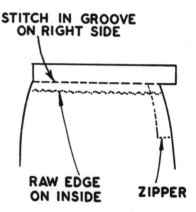

STITCH IN GROOVE ON RIGHT SIDE

RAW EDGE ON INSIDE   ZIPPER

Fig. 304. Stitching the belt.

C. Finish the inside edge of the belt.
  1. Turn down the underside of the belt. (This may have a selvage or a cut edge. Do not turn under the cut edge or selvage).
  2. Baste into position just above the seamline.
  3. Turn the skirt to the right side and stitch by machine through all the thicknesses around the waistline in the seamline groove. Fasten the ends (Fig. 304).

  4. Trim back the interfacing to the line of stitching.
  5. If the inside ravels, overcast the edges, or use seam binding ribbon.
  6. Press.

This method of attaching a belt is very flat, wears well, and is used by the tailors. If one is accustomed to a satisfactory dressmaker's method, that method may be substituted for the one above.

CHAPTER 39

Hemming the Skirt

WHILE fashion decrees whether a skirt is long or short, you must be the person to determine the most flattering length for you. The professional-looking hem is even in depth, and properly finished so that the stitches or the outline of the hem do not show on the right side.

I. **Mark the hemline on the desired length. (If the skirt is on the bias, let it hang for 48 hours before marking the hemline.)**
A. Use a hem marker, either the pin or chalk type; or
B. Use a tailor's square. Put a rubber band around the marking at the desired length; or
C. Use a yardstick, holding it squarely in a vertical position.
D. If possible, the fitter should move around the one whose hem line is being established, rather than have her move.
E. Stand with the weight evenly distributed on both feet.
F. Put in pins parallel to the floor 3 or 4 in. apart.

II. **Lay the skirt on a table to pin up and baste the hem.**
A. Match the side seams, center front, and center back. Pin up the hem at these points.
B. Place the pins vertically, close to the edge to define the hem fold (Fig. 306).
C. If there is any irregularity in the hemline as it is marked, allow the hemline to run as it "wants to," rather than force it to turn where it is marked.
D. Baste along the hem-fold edge, correcting any evidence of twist in the fabric between the pins (Fig. 306).

III. **Trim the hem to the desired width.**
A. Using a gauge (cardboard or metal), trim the hem evenly to the desired depth.
B. Recommended depths are:
 1. For a circular skirt — 1½ in. or less.
 2. For a straight skirt — 2 to 2½ in.

IV. **Remove fullness in the hem.**
A. Run a machine basting or small running stitch ¼ in. from the cut edge of the hem. Pull up the thread so the hem falls fairly flat in even gathers between the seams (Fig. 307).

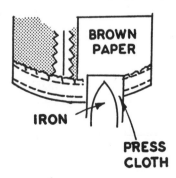

BROWN
PAPER

IRON

PRESS
CLOTH

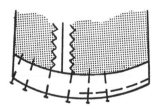

Fig. 306. Pinning the hem.

Fig. 307. Removing fullness.

B. In wool, shrink out the fullness with steam, gliding the iron from the fold inward. Use a piece of brown paper under the hem allowance while shrinking and pressing to prevent imprints (Fig. 307).

V. **Finish the upper edge of the hem.**

A. A seam binding finish is classic for wools and blends. Open the hem flat on the machine and lap the binding over the raw edge about ⅛ in., easing the binding onto the wool. Turn up the hem and fasten by hand. *Bias tape may be used on gored skirts.* Sew the tape, which has been shaped on the gathering line with the machine-stitching either flat onto the hem or inside the fold of the tape. You may machine-stitch the folded edge with a lengthened stitch and draw up lightly. Hand-hem.

B. On jersey and other wools, pink the raw edge and machine-stitch ¼ in. from the edge. After pinking the raw edge, baste the hem to the garment ½ to ⅜ in. from the pinked edge. Fold the garment back along the basting and do the running catch stitch along the fold, catching the hem to the garment. The folded edge will spring back. Top-press and flatten with a beater.

C. *Bound* hems are used on fabrics which ravel easily. Bind the raw edge of the hem with seam tape or folded bias. Fold and stitch over the raw seam edge with the wider part of the binding on the underside. Slip-stitch the hem fold of the binding invisibly or fold back the hem fold and slip-stitch at the machine-stitching line on the underside.

VI. **Hand-stitch the hem.**

A. The *tailor's hem* is a fast method. Fold the hem back and catch a few threads on the hem and then on the garment. Tailors call this a running catch stitch (Fig. 308).

Fig. 308. A tailor's hem.

B. *Hand-hemming visible on the inside* (slip-stitched) is done by taking a thread or two on the outside and then in the fold or tape (Fig. 309).

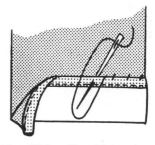

Fig. 309. Hand-hemming.

NOTE: A tailor's hem may be made with a taped hem by folding the tape back and making a running catch stitch between the hem and the garment (Fig. 229C, p. 110).

C. A *blind-stitched hem* is one of the least visible of the hand-stitched hems. Run the needle inside of the fold and then catch a thread or two of the garment (Fig. 310).

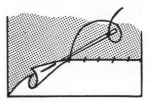

Fig. 310. A blind-stitched hem.

D. *Catch-stitched hems* are worked from left to right at an even slant. This is

a very durable hem, but more conspicuous (Fig. 311).

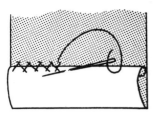

Fig. 311.   A catch-
stitched hem.

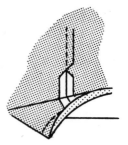

Fig. 312.   Clipping the
seam at the top of hem.

VII. Clip skirt hems with pleats.

A. Clip the seam in firm materials at
the top of the hem and press it open
from the clip to the bottom (Fig.
312). Trim the seam in the hem to
about ¼ in. In heavy fabrics, clip a
notch out of the seam edge at the
foldline. To facilitate pressing, one
may stitch close to the fold of the
hem on the wrong side either by
machine or by hand.

B. In materials which ravel, do not clip
above hem. Open the seam under
the hem, and turn gradually above
the hemline.

VIII. Press the hem.

A. Press on a well-padded surface.
B. Press or "pat" the hem; do not
"push" or iron it.
C. Press from the hemline toward the
top of the garment, never around the
edge.

CHAPTER 40

Applying Belt Fasteners

BUTTONS and buttonholes, snaps, or hooks and eyes are the most common fasteners used for belt closures.

Snaps are used as an invisible fastener where there is little strain. They may be used on an underlap or overlap of a belt where the strain is secured by a button or hook and eye.

Hooks and eyes are used where there is more strain. A straight eye or thread loop is utilized for a more inconspicuous closing. A small "sew-on" pants hook and eye is excellent for wool skirts since the hook does not snag the material as with the traditional hook and eye.

For directions for sewing on buttons, see Chapter 32, p. 128.

Hooks and Eyes

I. Mark the location.

A. During fitting, lap the belt to the position at which it will be worn and mark.

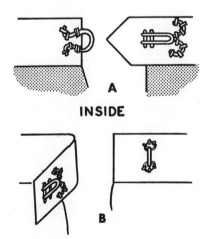

A

INSIDE

B

Fig. 316.   Hooks and eyes.

B. Mark the exact location of the fastener with a pin, chalk, or basting thread.

II. Choose the proper kind of hook and eye for the location in which it is to be used.

A. A *round eye* is used on the underside of the belt at the edge of the underlap with the eye protruding (Fig. 316, a).

B. A *straight eye* is used when the hook is placed ⅛ to 1⁄16 in. from the edge of the cloth on the underside of the overlap and the eye on the right side of the belt. The straight (bar) eye should meet the curved turning end of the hook (Fig. 316, b).

C. Sizes 2 and 3 are most commonly used for wool garments.

III. Sew on the hooks and eyes.

A. Use matching waxed hand-sewing silk, heavy-duty thread (sewing), silk thread, or buttonhole twist.

B. After the hook and eye is placed in the proper position, secure the thread under the hook with two to three over-and-over stitches.

C. Sew around the eyes with an overhand or a buttonhole stitch. Be sure you do not penetrate the right side of the garment.

D. Take several stitches under the end of the hook to keep it flat against the garment.

E. Fasten the thread with several over-and-over stitches. Run the threads between the layers of fabric, and clip them close to the fabric.

IV. Make thread loops, if desired.
A. Thread loops may be substituted for a straight (bar) eye. The former are more inconspicuous.
B. Make a strand using two to three strands of buttonhole twist or waxed hand-sewing silk, or four strands of sewing silk. Anchor the ends with over-and-over stitches (see "Swing tack," p. 37).
C. Blanket-stitch or buttonhole-stitch over the strands, keeping the stitches close together.
D. Fasten the first and last stitches into the belt to give added strength and to hide the over-and-over stitches.

Snaps

l. Mark the location.
A. Same as I above.

II. Choose the proper size snaps and locate them correctly.
A. Snaps come in many sizes. Select the proper size for the weight of your material. Sizes 2/0 and 3/0 are most commonly used for skirt belts.
B. Choose the color which will be most inconspicuous on your garment.

III. Sew on snaps.
A. See step III, A, above for the choice of thread.
B. Sew the ball to the overlap of the belt first.
C. The socket (which clasps the ball) is placed on the right side of the underlap.
D. If the round-eye closure is used, place a snap at the end of the overlap. If a straight eye is used, and a hook is placed at the end of the overlap, the snap is located at the end of the underlap.
E. Fasten the thread with over-and-over stitches under the snap and take three or four stitches in each hole of the snap or buttonhole stitch. Slide the needle from one hole in the snap to the other. Fasten the thread with two or three tiny over-and-over stitches.

CHAPTER 41

Characteristics of the Garment With a "Custom Look"

YOUR strictly tailored garment, whether it is completely hand-tailored, machine-tailored, or a combination of the two, should possess the "custom look." Let us review the qualities of this kind of garment.

The Coat

I. General fit of the coat.
A. It should be a smooth, loose fit without diagonal or pulled lines, especially over the waist and hip areas.
1. A straight coat barely touches the hips.
2. A full coat does not touch the hips.
B. Soft folds (blade of fabric) fall vertically.
1. From the armscye at the front.
2. From the armscye at the back.
C. Shoulders are smooth and free from wrinkles.
D. There is a curve from the bust to the armscye.
E. There is a slight curve in the back from the shoulder to the armscye.
F. The curve or corner at the bottom of the coat front lies smooth without turning outward.
G. The seams of the front edge are rolled under slightly, are flat, even, and hang straight.
H. The roll line from the collar to the top button fits snugly against the body.

II. Grainline and fabric design.
A. Filling (crosswise) yarns are parallel to the floor across the center front at the bustline, across the back, and across the sleeve at the bustline.
B. Warplines (lengthwise) are perpendicular to the floor at the center front and center back. The line is vertical at the center of the sleeve when viewed from the side.
C. Plaids or patterns should be carried out across the garment, openings, and sleeves as planned.

III. Collar.
A. The collar creaseline fits snugly across the back but not too tight over the top of the shoulder and at the sides. (If there is weight here, the shoulder seam does not fit on the shoulder, or the undercollar is not attached properly.)
B. The collar edge is pressed smoothly with no seam showing.
C. The fall of the collar lies smoothly against the undercollar and the coat. The "fall" should be longer than the stand to cover it.

IV. Lapels.
A. Lapels roll back softly along the creaseline without an actual crease being pressed.
B. The points or edges lie smoothly in position without curling.
C. The seamlines do not show, but are rolled under slightly.

V. Sleeves.
A. The warp yarns (lengthwise) from the shoulder to the elbow are perpendicular to the floor.

B. The sleeve fits smoothly into the armscye.

C. The bottom of the sleeve is well pressed and a little longer at the back of the wrist than at the front.

D. From the elbow to the wrist the sleeve is shaped to follow the armline.

E. The hem of the sleeve is invisible.

VI. Hemline.

A. The hemline is inconspicuous and even.

B. There are no drawn lines caused by "lining pull."

VII. Buttons, buttonholes, pockets, and interfacings.

A. The buttons are well chosen for the garment and sewed on with the proper shank.

B. The buttonholes are evenly spaced, they are the proper length for the buttons, and they are nicely made.

C. The pockets are evenly spaced, well made, and pressed flat.

D. The interfacings are flat and inconspicuous.

The Skirt

I. General fit.

A. The center front and center back warp yarns (lengthwise) are perpendicular to the floor.

B. The side seams are perpendicular to the floor.

C. The skirt fits smoothly with ease.

II. Seams.

A. The seamlines are straight and well pressed, but no imprints show on the right side.

B. The seams are finished properly and are even in width.

III. Skirt band.

A. The skirt band is even in width, well pressed, and stitched straight.

B. The grainline is straight at the ends. There is sufficient overlap and it is finished properly with appropriate fasteners.

IV. Slide fastener (zipper).

A. The slide fastener should match the fabric in color and weight.

B. It is evenly stitched, concealed, and smooth.

V. Darts, pleats.

A. The darts are tapered properly, evenly spaced, and shaped at the ends.

B. The pleats are properly stitched and pressed.

C. There are no imprints on the right side from overpressing.

VI. Hem.

A. The hem is even in width and inconspicuous, with any fullness removed by shrinking onto tape.

B. Seam allowances that are in pleats are clipped at the hem so they lie smoothly.

C. The seam tape is stitched evenly and smoothly.

D. The seams inside the hem are pressed open.

E. The seamlines of the hem meet the seamlines in the skirt (sides and gores).

VII. Lining.

A. The lining is of a firm material, matched to the fabric in color.

B. It is long enough to reach below the hip when the wearer is sitting.

C. The lining is slightly snugger than the skirt.

D. The lining is fastened smoothly.

CHAPTER 42

Constructing and Applying Shields

(Dress Shields and Reinforcement Shields)

SHIELDS are placed under the arm in suit jackets or coats, either to protect from perspiration or to provide added wearability to the garment.

To protect from perspiration, one may purchase a ready-made rubberized shield and tack it at the corners and underarm seam. If the covering on the ready-made shield does not match the lining, it may be covered with lining material.

To Cover a Ready-Made Detachable Shield

I. Lay the ready-made shield on the lining fabric.

The widest part of the shield should be on the warpwise grain.

II. Cut the pieces of lining.

A. Cut four pieces for each section of the shield (two sections).

B. Cut the pieces the shape of the shield plus a seam allowance.

III. Cover the shield with the lining.

A. With the right sides together, stitch the curved armscye seam of the shield for each section.

B. Place the shield inside of the lining, turning under the seam allowance toward the inside around the lower edge.

C. You may blanket-stitch by hand with matching thread, or stitch by machine close to the edge, catching both sides.

IV. Attach the shield to the suit or coat.

A. Place one section of the shield inside the sleeve at the armscye and the other on the coat, with the bulk of the shield slightly toward the front of the garment.

B. Tack at the seamline and at points both on the coat side and in the sleeve.

To Make Reinforcement Shields

A reinforcement shield, used for added wearability, is more often found on men's sport coats and blazer coats for women. They are of two types: the first, stitched onto the body lining; and the second, made double of lining material or single of wool and stitched into the lining-sleeve seam and tacked at the body seamline.

Shield Stitched Onto Coat Lining

I. Stitch the underarm seam of the coat lining (before attaching it to the coat).

Stitch the seam and press it open.

II. Cut the reinforcement.

Using the armscye line as a guide, cut matching lining fabric the shape of the armscye and flush with the seam allowance. On the other edges,

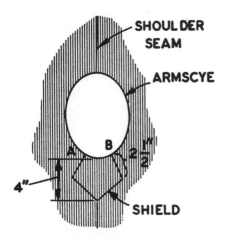

Fig. 319. A shield stitched
on a coat lining.

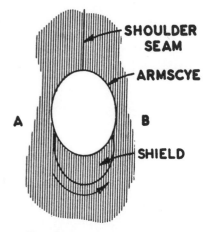

Fig. 320. A shield stitched
into a seam.

from A to B, provide a ½-in. seam
allowance. Cut two pieces (Fig. 319).

III. Attach it to the lining.

A. Turn under the seam allowance on
all the edges except the armscye line.
B. Place the wrong side of the shield
against the right side of the coat
lining.
C. Baste and stitch it into position.
D. At the armscye line attach the shield
to the seam allowance of the coat,
using a backstitch or machine stitch.

Shield Stitched Into Lining Seam

I. See step I above, "Shield Stitched
Onto Coat Lining."

II. Cut the shield.

A. Cut a double thickness of lining, or
a single layer of wool, shaped at the
armscye. From A to B in Figure 320
it is curved like a dress shield only

about 2½ to 3 in. deep and 5 in.
wide finished. Allow for seams.
B. Cut four pieces if lining is used, and
two pieces if wool is used.

III. Make the shield.

A. If lining is used, place the two right
sides together and stitch from A to
B in Figure 321, left. Turn and press.
B. If wool is used, bind the single edge
from A to B in Figure 321, right.

Fig. 321. Making the shield.

IV. Attach the shield to the lining.

A. Attach the shield to the lining on
the seam allowance at the armscye.
B. Tack the shield to the lining at the
bottom on the seamline.

CHAPTER 43

The Short-Cut Tailoring Technique

IN THE past few years, there have been dressmakers and teachers of clothing promoting a type of tailoring called, "Short-Cut Tailoring." The pioneer and leader in this field is Edna Bryte Bishop. As Educational Director for Advance Pattern Company, she has published a leaflet "Bishop Method of Clothing Construction — 9 Learnings," which contains a section on tailoring. Later, the Extension Departments of some states published circulars using this method. Two examples of the latter are: "How to Make a Coat" by Dodson and Reis and "Here's How to Tailor" by Lucille Rea.

The advantages in utilizing the short-cut tailoring method are: it is much less time consuming than custom tailoring; it requires less skill in manipulation; and, it may be used at home with little formal classroom instruction. Many educators believe that it is well for the high school student in home economics classes or the adult beginner, to commence with this type of tailoring before progressing to custom tailoring.

In short-cut tailoring, machine pad-stitching is employed, tape or shaped strip is applied to the interfacing before it is attached to the garment, interfacings are seamed by machine, little shaping of cloth is required, and the collar is applied leaving the ends and notch of the collar open — later closing them by the use of directional stitching. Sometimes the undercollar is attached to the coat, the upper collar to the facing, and then the coat is stitched up the facing, around the outer edge of the collar and down the other side. On children's and boxy coats, the entire lining, including the sleeves, may be stitched in by machine.

Although the garment produced by short-cut tailoring is not quite the same in appearance as the one produced by custom tailoring, short-cut tailoring does have its place in home sewing today. It is particularly well suited for making children's garments or summer suits which are not worn long enough to justify the time spent in custom tailoring. Boxy, lightly fitted suits are also adaptable, for they usually do not require intricate shaping.

CHAPTER 44

Buying a Tailored Garment

NEARLY every woman who has tailored a suit or coat will remark, "Now, I'll know what to look for in a ready-made garment." Another remark frequently heard is, "I know now why custom-tailored garments seem so expensive."

There are a few tips that may assist you in selecting your new coat or suit if you are buying a ready-made garment.

I. Amount of money to spend.

A. Shop at a store with a reputation for good quality.

B. Beware of bargain prices, because in coats the hidden values affect wearability.

C. Simple styles often have more wear per dollar than "high"-styled garments of the season.

II. Becoming styles for the individual.

A. Tall, slim figure.
1. Full coat.
2. Double-breasted.
3. Longer jacket.
4. Man-tailored if it suits your personality.
5. High collar for a long neck.
6. Short, wide revers.
7. Full, bulky sleeves.
8. Dolman and raglan sleeves for square shoulders.
9. Straight skirt; it may have slits.

B. Heavy or short figure.
1. Straight, full-length; or
2. Slightly flared.
3. Princess lines.
4. Single-breasted.

5. Shorter jacket.
6. Long, narrow revers.
7. Fitted sleeve.
8. Set-in sleeves for sloping shoulders.
9. Skirt with a slight flare or low pleats.

C. Generally speaking, a suit that can be worn with a variety of blouses, sweaters and jewelry is more versatile.

III. Color that is practical.

A. Choose a color that is becoming to you and fits in with your wardrobe.

B. Plain, basic colored fabrics (beige or gray), often give more wear for a limited wardrobe.

C. Consider whether the color will soil easily or show lint.

IV. Warmth characteristics.

A. For cold climates.
1. Full-length, belted coat.
2. Buttoned front.
3. High collar that buttons close at the neck.
4. Wrist or sleeve guards.

B. Zip-in liner coats offer wear for all-season wear.

V. Judging fit.

Refer to Chapter 41, p. 153.

VI. Judging workmanship.

A. A high-quality suit is cut on the grain and stitched with matching silk thread.

B. The ends of the buttonholes and pocket corners should be well fastened and reinforced.

C. If lining seems to fray, check the width of the seam edge.

D. The lining should be tacked securely to the garment at shoulder, side seams, and armholes, and have a ¾ to 1 in. allowance at the back.

E. The lining and interlining should be seamed separately, and the lining should cover the interlining at the lower edge.

F. The word "hand-tailored" is not an indication of quality. The handwork may be poorly done. Sometimes good machine work looks and wears better than poor handwork. Often the qual- ity of hand processes is hidden in handwork around armscye, shoulder, and neck.

VII. **Trimmings.**

A. The cost of fur-trimmed coats is higher and the cost of upkeep is greater than an all-cloth garment. If fur trim is selected, be sure that it is thick and soft, with no weak spots.

B. Check to see that the buttons have smooth edges, and slip in and out of buttonholes without straining the buttonhole.

WARDROBE PLANNING GUIDE

This guide may help you decide which type of garment you need in your wardrobe. List the dresses and suits you have. Fill in accessories you have to go with them. Some garments may fit into one or more categories.

Basic Costumes	Suits	Dresses	Coats	Hats	Gloves Handbag Accessories	Need to Make	Need to Buy
For city wear							
Luncheon meetings							
Church							
For casual wear							
Night school							
Teas							
Parties							
Others							

Selected Bibliography

BOOKS

Bane, Allyne. *Tailoring.* New York: Mc-Graw-Hill Book Co., 1958.

Beck, Doris May. *Custom Tailoring for Homemakers.* Peoria, Illinois: Chas. A. Bennett Co., 1964.

Donielson, Dorothy, and Pond, June. *Tailoring for Women Step by Step.* San Jose, California: Hallen Publishing Co., 1963.

Goodman, Bonnie. *Tailoring for the Family.* New York: Prentice-Hall, Inc., 1951.

Mansfield, Evelyn. *Clothing Construction.* Boston: Houghton Mifflin Co., 1953.

Mauck, Frances F. *Modern Tailoring for Women.* New York: The Macmillan Co., 1947.

Poulin, Clarence. *Tailoring Suits the Professional Way.* Peoria: Chas. A. Bennett Co., Inc., 1952.

Strickland, Gertrude. *A Tailoring Manual.* New York: The Macmillan Co., 1956.

BULLETINS

Bishop, Edna Bryte. *The Bishop Method of Clothing Construction — 9 learnings.* New York: Advance Pattern Co., Inc., 1955.

———— *The Bishop Method of Clothing Construction — Pattern Alterations for the Majority.* New York: Advance Pattern Co., Inc., 1957.

Carter, Isabel. *Vogue Dressmaking Book.* New York: The Conde'Nast Publications, Inc., 1953.

Dodson, Ethelwyn, and Quinn, Frances Reis. *How to Make a Coat.* Circular 419. University of California: Agricultural Publications Office, 1953.

Let's Sew with Wool. New York: The Wool Bureau, Inc., 1956.

Lund, Belinda. *Cut to Fit Handbook.* Green Bay: Privately printed, 1954.

Rea, Lucille. *Here's How to Tailor.* Ames, Iowa: State College, Agricultural Extension Service, 1950.

Scopelle, Marie L., and Curtin, Kathryn. *Butterick-New Sewing Book.* New York: The Butterick Company, Inc., 1956.

Scott, Clarice L. *Buying Women's Coats and Suits.* Home and Garden Bulletin No. 31. Washington, D. C.: U. S. Government Printing Office, 1954.

———— *Men's Suits — How to Judge Quality.* Home and Garden Bulletin No. 54. Washington, D. C.: U. S. Government Printing Office, 1957.

Smith, Margaret. *Coat Making at Home.* U. S. Department of Agriculture Farmers Bulletin No. 1894. Washington, D. C.: U. S. Government Printing Office, 1941.

———— *Fitting Coats and Suits.* Home and Garden Bulletin No. 11. Washington, D. C.: U. S. Government Printing Office, 1952.

———— *How to Tailor a Woman's Suit.* Home and Garden Bulletin No. 20. Washington, D. C.: U. S. Government Printing Office, 1956.

———— *Pattern Alteration.* Farmers' Bulletin No. 1968. Washington, D. C.: U. S. Government Printing Office, 1948.

Sources of Materials

TAILORING SUPPLIES

1. Newark Dressmaker Supply Co.
   140 Halsey St.
   Newark, New Jersey 07102
2. Jos. Arenson & Sons (School orders)
   1026 W. Winnebago
   Milwaukee, Wis. 53205
3. "J and J" Tailoring Supplies (Individual
   retail orders)
   5506 Goucher Lane
   Monona, Wis. 53716

WOVEN LABELS

1. Bussard's Garment Labels
   P.O. Box 2264
   Portland, Oregon 97214

PLEATING LENGTHS OF MATERIALS FOR SKIRTS

1. Artistic Designs
   260 W. 39th St.
   New York, N. Y. 10018

WOOL CLOTH

1. Harris Woolen Co.
   1080 W. Adams
   Chicago, Ill.
2. English Woolen Mills (also tailoring
   supplies)
   812 N. 3rd St.
   Milwaukee, Wis.
3. Welek Fabrics
   1204 Washington Ave.
   St. Louis, Mo. 63103
4. Amluxen's
   913 Nicollet Ave.
   Minneapolis 2, Minn.
5. Homestead Woolen Mills, Inc.
   West Swanzey
   New Hampshire (Mill Store)
6. Amana Society
   Woolen Mill Salesroom
   Amana, Iowa
7. Kovack Fabric Center
   630 N. Broadway
   Milwaukee, Wisconsin
8. J. L. Hudson Co.
   Detroit, Mich.

Index